BASS COOKBOOK

A. D. Livingston

STACKPOLE
BOOKS

Copyright © 1996 by A. D. Livingston

Published by
STACKPOLE BOOKS
5067 Ritter Road
Mechanicsburg, PA 17055

Printed in the United States of America

Cover design by Mark Olszewski with Caroline M. Miller

First Edition

10 9 8 7 6 5 4 3 2 1

Other Stackpole books by A. D. Livingston: *Venison Cookbook; Wild Turkey Cookbook; Trout Cookbook.*

Library of Congress Cataloging-in-Publication Data

Livingston, A. D., 1932–
    Bass cookbook / A. D. Livingston. — 1st ed.
        p.   cm.
    Includes index.
    ISBN 0-8117-2509-X
    1. Cookery (Bass)   I. Title.
TX748.B37.L58   1996
641.6′92—dc20   95-35528
                                                                                     CIP

Portions of this book were previously published, in a slightly different form, in the author's regular column in *Gray's Sporting Journal* and in articles that first appeared in *Sports Afield*. The author is indebted to many writers, sportsmen, cooks, and friends—all of whom are appro-priately acknowledged in the text—and to his family, who provided the fish and helped test the recipes.

CONTENTS

INTRODUCTION

Anyone who puzzles over the sharp differences in regional cooking and grapples with culinary prejudices from place to place in this small world should go back and take a look at the American Indians. The Chinook of the Northwest, for example, lived mostly on fish and shellfish from the sea, whereas the Apache of the Southwest had no stomach whatsoever for fish. Nor did the Apache enjoy banding together and chasing buffalo all over the plains like the Sioux. They were lone hunters who liked to roam the foothills stalking deer, their favorite food, one on one. The Apache also ate rabbits, wood rats, and other good animals that feed on grass seeds, nuts, or grain, and they were fond of a few seed-eating birds, such as mourning doves and whitewings. But, surprisingly, they really didn't care for the wild turkey, which, they knew, fed extensively on worms or grubs, just as fish do. Of course, the Apache wouldn't eat the white man's nasty hogs and chickens, for the same reason.

Not far to the north of the Apaches, the Utes and the Paiutes enjoyed pretty much what they could find or dig, including lizards, grasshoppers, and grubs. Along the Atlantic seaboard, gigantic shell mounds attest to the Indians' love of oysters and clams—but some finicky tribes wouldn't touch the prolific mussel, although it was the same species that was so highly prized in France and England. The Indians along the Gulf Coast also ate lots of fish and shellfish, but studies of kitchen middens and shell mounds have shown that an ancient tribe near Fort Walton Beach in the Florida Panhandle didn't care for the mullet. Today, the white man holds an annual mullet festival at Boggy Bayou, not far from the Shell Mound Museum. Indeed, the mullet is a favorite fish today in most parts of Florida, as far west as Pensacola, where it is traditionally served up for breakfast. A scant two hundred miles away, however, the people of New Orleans don't put much stock in mullet—and certainly not for breakfast.

Knowing all this, I shouldn't have been taken aback some years ago by a letter I received from a well-known New York book editor who sometimes wrote for the outdoor trade. I had proposed, through a literary agency, a little book called *Cooking with Bass*. The editor wrote back rather uppishly that the black bass rates no higher than midway on a culinary scale of one to ten. That cultural shock hit me twenty-two years ago, but in more recent times this fellow saw fit to allow the black bass into his own cookbook. I couldn't believe my eyes! Is it mere coincidence that the bass has risen on the culinary scale as it became more and more popular as a sport fish, even in Maine? Or has the fish simply become too important commercially to snub entirely?

The editor did, however, have to stipulate in his book that the bass is pretty good table fare, as he had been told, provided that it is skinned. Skinned? Why? To get rid of the muddy taste. What muddy taste? I've never skinned a bass in my life, except to test out another cook's recipes or how-to methods, and I can say with a clear conscience, without having to jump onto the band wagon, that the black bass has always been my favorite all-around fish, even when I used to call it "green trout."

A lot of the talk about a muddy taste in bass seems to originate in the Northeast and from publishing outfits based in New York City. Clearly, opinion in high places is lined up against me. There are, however, other points of view that tend to support my stand. Here's one from *Cy Littlebee's Guide to Cooking Fish & Game:* "Folks down East talk about bass having a muddy flavor, too. Guess we're just luckier in Missouri. It can happen here though, when bass comes out of stagnating or muddy water. I never had much trouble myself, if I scraped the bass good and scrubbed the skin side in cold running water for a few minutes." It seems to me that Cy Littlebee made his stand clear—but he had to hedge a little, and count himself lucky, just in case New England bass really do taste muddy.

It would seem that bass from the state of Louisiana, which contains lots of midwestern mud that has washed down the Mississippi, ought to taste muddy if any of them do. Yet *The Frank Davis Seafood Notebook*, written and published in Louisiana, makes no mention of any sort of off flavor in the bass's skin or elsewhere, although he is quick to do so with some other fish. I admit that I have from time to time detected a slight off flavor in a bass or two, but I don't think it comes from mud or from the skin. The taste is quite localized, and I believe it comes either from a white lining inside the rib cage or from the small bloody masses attached to the bottom of the backbone inside the rib cage. In my experience, this taste almost always occurs in bass that have been cooked too long.

My conclusion in this matter is that some people are prejudiced, or else they simply don't know how to cook, or both. A third possibility is that they have been brainwashed. If anyone starts eating any fish with the fear that it's going to taste muddy, it probably will. The river-run channel catfish has long suffered in some quarters from the "mudcat" syndrome, which the catfish-farming industry has tried to exploit, with some success, in order to sell more pond-raised cats. Actually, there is no such species as the mudcat, although some of the several bullheads seem to prefer a muddy bottom. The infamous bowfin is often called a "mudcat"—but it's not a catfish at all. In some areas, the black bass may have been labeled "muddy" because some casual anglers haven't distinguished it from the rock bass, which can, when fried, have a somewhat musty taste that I suppose could be described as "muddy." In all fairness, however, I must add that some experts rate the rock bass and other warmouths as excellent table fare. So there you have it. One man's trash, another man's treasure. In view of the truth of that maxim, I can only hope that this little book will at last set the bass free, culinarily speaking, in the minds of all honest men everywhere.

Most American anglers won't have much trouble with the term *bass*, although they might argue among themselves about the relative merits of the spotted bass, Kentucky bass, largemouth, smallmouth, redeye, and so on. People who read cookbooks and shop at the market instead of catching their own may have a problem because so many different kinds of saltwater fish are called bass of one sort or another, and very few general cookbooks mean freshwater black bass when they call for bass or even black bass. Although these cookbook bass vary from 2 pounds to 500, most of them are good eating and have a mild, white, lean flesh that flakes easily. Happily, most of the recipes in this book can be used for both freshwater and sea basses. I'll try to sort out what's what in appendix B.

In appendix A, I set forth ten basic steps to help the sportsman and the cook put better bass on the table. Good fishing—and good eating.

—A. D. Livingston

ONE

Fried Bass
and Hush Puppies

For crunch and flavor, frying is one of the best ways to cook bass, as well as other fish with mild, white flesh. Unfortunately, however, many people frown on fried foods these days. There is some justification to the charges that too much fat isn't good for your health, but it could also be true that the amount of fat in properly fried foods is overestimated. Frying at a high temperature and without using a thick batter will reduce the amount of fat that is soaked up by the fish, and the use of vegetable oils instead of animal fats for frying reduces the cholesterol. Properly draining the fried fish also reduces the fat.

On the other hand, be warned that my favorite recipe and technique produces fried fish so good that most people tend to eat far too much of it, thereby increasing their fat intake. Further, fried potatoes and hush puppies—required eating for a genuine fish fry in some quarters—also increase one's intake of fat. Anyone who can't control himself should perhaps skip this chapter and go directly to poached fish. On the other hand, remember that poached fish piled high with a thick sauce might indeed have *more* fat than fried fish.

In any case, attention to details of cooking and the quality of the basic ingredients for frying—fish, cornmeal, and cooking oil—are important.

Cooking Oil. Some of the old-time recipes specify beef suet or hog lard for frying fish, and others hold out for bacon drippings. If used correctly, these animal fats can produce very good fried fish, but these days the trend is toward the cholesterol-free vegetable oils. I have tried just about everything, but years ago I settled on peanut oil for several reasons. It has a high smoke point; it is tasteless and doesn't absorb odors as readily as other oils; and with proper care, it can be used again and again. I have used corn oil extensively and have experimented with canola oil, sunflower oil, and various blends, but I always come back to peanut oil for serious skillet frying and for deep frying.

Sautéing requires only a small amount of oil on the skillet or griddle. Olive oil and clarified butter are good for sautéing, and some people even get by with some sort of spray-on oil. Still other people mix butter and beef suet, and swear by it. As a rule, trout is more often sautéed than bass is, and often in trout cookery the small amount of butter or oil left in the skillet is used as the base for a sauce to be poured over the fish. The same technique can be used in bass cookery. See chapter 2 for some recipes of this sort.

Frying in a skillet requires more oil than sautéing does, and the oil can be reused. Filling a deep fryer with a gallon or two of oil becomes an expensive proposition if you don't reuse it.

To save the oil, let it cool somewhat, carefully pour it off the bottom dredgings, then strain it. Running it through a coffee filter system is ideal; merely use the plastic cage from an old coffee maker and new paper filters. This takes lots of time, and several runs will be required to filter all the oil used in a large deep fryer, but the clean, clear reusable oil is worth the trouble. You can speed up the process by changing filters from time to time.

You can "freshen" oil by frying potatoes in it. I also like to add two or three slices of ginger root to old oil to give it a nice smell and a clean taste. In fact, I will sometimes leave the ginger root in the oil while I fry the fish. When frying fish, part of the coating or batter (especially with cornmeal) will come off in bits and accumulate on the bottom. If you are frying a very large quantity of fish and hush puppies, it's good to devise a fine strainer to get some of it out.

Be warned that hot cooking oil is dangerous. Believe me, I have smoked up more than one house because I forgot a skillet half full of grease on a stove. Overheated oil will actually catch on fire, and it is dangerous. I have heard of several houses burning to the ground because of a kitchen grease fire. Unless you have a fire extinguisher especially for grease fires, your best bet is to sprinkle or toss some baking soda into the skillet; this will very quickly produce carbon dioxide, which will smother the fire almost instantly. I always keep two or three boxes of the stuff in the kitchen so that I will have it if needed. You can also extinguish the fire by placing a lid on the skillet. As an initial precaution, take the telephone off the hook while you're frying the fish and hush puppies.

Never use water on a grease fire. If you can't put out the fire, I recommend that you let it burn instead of trying to take it out into the yard. More than one person has been seriously burned by picking up the skillet and running for the door. This is very risky. Opening the door can cause a draft, blowing the flames back at you. Dropping the skillet can also cause burns and spread the fire.

In case of fire, shut all the doors to keep the smoke confined to the kitchen. (As a precaution, you may want to call the fire department.) After the flame is out, open the windows. Your homeowner's insurance should pay for repainting.

Some patio deep fryers are also dangerous, partly because they hold so much oil. Never use them in an area where children or good ol' boys are playing.

Skillets and Cookers. There are all manner of fish cookers from which to choose, but an ordinary skillet is hard to beat if you have only a few people to feed. I prefer heavy-duty cast-iron skillets. Others, such as thick aluminum, can be used, but keep in mind that bass is best fried on high heat, which is not good for some of the thin metal skillets with ceramic or teflon coatings. Electric skillets sometimes come in handy, but I usually reach for my 10½-inch cast-iron skillet. (The size of the skillet is the diameter as measured across the bottom.) Sometimes I'll use

3

two such skillets—one for fish and one for hush puppies or potatoes.

There are several 3- or 4-inch deep cast-iron or aluminum fish cookers available. Some of these are round and can be used atop a stove burner; others are oblong and require a source of heat on each end. Most of these do a very good job, provided that you can heat them properly. Some small camp stoves simply won't get a cast-iron Dutch oven half full of grease hot enough to cook bass according to Livingston.

Some of the best deep fryers I have ever seen are designed to be used on the patio and are heated by a large portable gas tank. These are nice to have whenever you have lots of fish to fry. They can be taken to camp if you can drive in, and some of the best bass I've ever eaten were cooked in one of these deep fryers on the tailgate of a pickup truck parked under a bridge. They can also be taken along on pontoon boats and other craft, but remember that hot grease is very dangerous.

All large deep fryers should have a thermometer. Some come with thermometers mounted on the side, but you may have to rig one for yourself. Keep the oil temperature at least 375 degrees, preferably higher. At lower temperatures, the fish are likely to become tough and chewy and will soak up too much grease.

I have a deep fryer that fits atop the grilling side of my kitchen stove, and I sometimes use it to advantage. It's not as large as a patio fryer, but it will do a good job if it is heated hot enough. I also use it from time to time to cook whole fish that are too large for a skillet. In fact, while writing these pages, I fried a whole bass of about 2½ pounds, head on, for a Chinese sweet-and-sour recipe (page 14). It was delicious.

Some griddles can also be used to fry fish, but these hold very little oil and the frying is of a different sort. I really prefer to have the oil almost as deep as the fish are thick, although using a griddle with only a small amount of hot oil is much better than deep frying in oil that isn't hot enough. If you use a griddle, you'll have to fry on a lower heat so that the outside of the fish won't burn before the inside gets done. (With deeper oil, the oil itself does part of the cooking.) If I cook on a griddle at reduced heat, I consider the fish to be sautéed instead of fried, although I may not call it that. Small trout are often cooked by this technique and are very good. But for bass, a fish with low oil content, I prefer outright frying. On the other hand, I have eaten some very good bass fillets cooked in a little butter on a griddle; often, after cooking, I'll make a sauce from the browned butter left on the griddle, merely stirring in a little lemon juice and chopped parsley.

You can also stir-fry fish successfully in a wok, but bass fingers tend to break up if they are stirred very much. Try chunks instead of fingers, put quite a bit of oil in the wok, and reduce the stirring. You can pour out some of the oil before stir-frying the vegetables.

Strainers, Brown Bags, and Other Accessories. For skillet frying, I always use tongs to place the fish into hot oil, to turn them, and to remove them. I like short, spring-loaded tongs because they are easy to use and have a sure grip. Large tongs with claw fingers tend to tear tender fillets. I seldom use a spatula or a fork for this purpose, unless I can't find my tongs.

For deep frying, the so-called french fry strainers, designed to fit down into the oil container, are nice, but I seldom use them. They tend to overload the deep fryer when they are first immersed, thereby lowering the temperature drastically. If you do wish to use a strainer, heat it in the oil before loading it with fish or potatoes, or leave it immersed in the oil and put the fish or potatoes in a few at a time. Then use the strainer to take out the whole batch.

Instead of a large strainer for fries, I prefer to use a hand-held strainer or skimmer to dip them out. I drain the strainer a little over the fryer, then put the potatoes onto a brown bag. I think they drain better this way instead of piled on top of each other in a batch strainer.

Draining fried fish is a very important step. I like to put down two large grocery bags, one atop the other, beside my skillet or fryer. I remove the fish with tongs, one piece at a time, and place it on the brown bag. For preliminary draining, I place each piece directly onto the brown paper, not piled onto another piece. I leave the first batch spread out while cooking the second batch. Then I move the first batch down, forming a pile on one end and thereby making room for spreading out the second batch. For up to six people, the fish and hush puppies, and maybe even fried potatoes, can be put onto a single bag. I serve the fish and bread simply by putting the whole bag onto the table, usually on a tray or, better, on a wooden cutting block of suitable size.

If you are cooking lots of fish or a combination of potatoes, fish, and hush puppies, remember that you can use more than one brown bag. When cooking several batches in a single skillet, you can keep the cooked fish warm by covering them with a brown bag.

You may want to use pretty paper towels to drain your fish and bread. Brown paper bags are better, but suit yourself. I'll have to admit, however, that brown bags aren't as good as they used to be. Some of them tear easily, and they don't seem to soak up as much grease. I understand that some of the modern brown bags are made from recycled paper, and I can't argue with that.

Coatings and Batters. M. F. K. Fisher, author of several cookbooks, once said, "One of the great troubles about most fried fish in America (that is honest fried fish, and not the sickening batter-coated monstrosity often sold in even reputable restaurants), is that it is overdone." It's true that one of the worst things you can do to a fish is to fry it too long. I also agree, up to a point, with the parenthetical comment about batter-coated fish. The late Waverley Root, author of *Food*, also disliked thick batters and accused inexpert British cooks of deep-frying in a batter with an overdose of flour, which, he says, makes the fish taste like library paste. Most of the thick batters taste all right to me, if they have crunch. But I really prefer the taste of bass fillets. Consequently, I *never* use a batter except when I am testing another person's recipe—or when I don't have enough fish to feed everybody. A simple dusting of cornmeal, or some other suitable coating, is less trouble, much cheaper, a good deal less messy, easier to fry, easier to drain, and less greasy.

Some of the recipes below call for batter for those who like it, but my best recommendation is that the fish be dusted with fine or extra-fine cornmeal made from whole-grain corn. The meal I have in mind is stone ground at a low grinding temperature. Since it contains the germ and all the oils, the meal has a limited shelf life. For this reason, the larger milling companies got away from it some years ago so that they wouldn't have to worry about outdated meals.

Fortunately, a few small mills stayed in business in various parts of the country, so the real stuff can still be purchased. (In fact, it seems to be making a comeback.) Most small millers, like local bakers, don't go through large regional food wholesalers; instead, they bring their product to the stores and rotate the stock. Note that the shelf life is extended by refrigeration or freezing. I buy meal in 10-pound bags and freeze it until needed.

If you don't know what I'm talking about and want to try some really good cornmeal, you may be able to find some in your local supermarket. Look for a rather quaint package, often in brown or yellow paper, with the words *stone-ground* or *water-ground style* on it. It may also have a date stamped on the package, either plain or in code. The meal is also available by mail order and possibly in health food stores, since it is whole-corn meal.

To work properly for fried fish, the cornmeal must be finely ground simply because the coarse stuff—and most of the meals made by large millers are downright gritty—won't stay on the fish without the aid of chicken eggs or goo of some sort. Extra-fine cornmeal works nicely as a coating, but it won't do for hush puppies, as they tend to pop open in the hot grease. I usually buy the fine grind so that I can use the same meal for both the fish and the hush puppies. Medium meal is best suited for corn bread that is to be baked in the oven.

I prefer white cornmeal, but yellow (or even purple) will also work if it is ground finely enough. Of course, the kind of corn that is used will have a bearing on the final product, just as different wheats make slightly different flours. If you can't find the stone-ground cornmeal, consider grinding your own from local corn—or from your own garden. Some good kitchen mills are available these days. In short, get some of this meal at any cost. It's simply better for the same reason that freshly ground peppercorns are better than bottled ground pepper. If you can't find the right stuff, try the Mexican *masa harina,* a tortilla meal made from corn. It's not quite the same thing, but it will do.

After you get the right stuff, put a little in a bag and shake the fish in it. I salt the fish before shaking it, but some people prefer to mix salt in with the meal. Suit yourself.

Plain flour also makes a good coating, but the result is different. I usually use it for frying fish that is to be covered with some sort of sauce. (See Sweet-and-Sour Bass recipe later in this chapter, for example.) I prefer flour for frying chicken or turkey fingers, and I won't hesitate to use plain flour for fish if I am out of the right sort of cornmeal. Flour also works well for pan-frying small fish in a little butter, a technique that is more or less traditional in trout cookery.

Other coatings can be used, such as chick-pea flour, a popular coating in Africa and the Middle East. Finely ground bread or cracker crumbs can also be used—including crushed corn flakes or even sugar-coated corn flakes—but some of these coatings are quick to burn, especially in a skillet where they are in direct contact with the bottom of the pan. I've seen all sorts of fish-fry mixtures on the market, some of which are highly seasoned. These are good, provided that the fish are fried properly.

I have tried all manner of coatings, and many exact combinations of ingredients, but I always come back to ordinary white cornmeal. Perhaps there is a deep-seated connection. At one time, grist mills were located along many small streams in this country, and often a single community had half a dozen mills within an easy buggy ride from town. Although most of these are now gone, the names of our roads indicate the location of many: Gilly Mill Road, Brunt Mill Road, and so on. At each mill was a millpond, which was usually available for fishing, especially by regular customers. Back then, these ponds were often the best fishing in the area. There were no large impoundments for hydroelectric power, flood control, or other uses; few state or municipal recreation lakes; and not many farm ponds. Hence, the millpond was a popular fishing hole and was the site of many a fish fry. Of course, having freshly caught fish along with freshly ground cornmeal for dusting the fish and making hush puppies produced some very good eating.

There are countless variations on the fried-fish theme, although I place basic ingredients and technique above the exact recipe. Here are a few recipes to try, starting with what I consider to be the simplest one. And the best.

A. D.'s Quintessential Bass

Because I have used this recipe in other books and in articles, I had to do some soul searching before using it again here. In the end, I came to realize that it is my duty as a food writer to repeat myself, simply because it is the best recipe in the world for fried fish and I would be cheating you if I withheld it.

I normally cook pan-dressed bass (from 1 to 2 pounds) with this recipe and technique, but fillets will also work. I don't use it for whole bass of any size, because the outside will burn before the inside is done.

> bass fillets
> fine white cornmeal, stone-ground
> peanut oil
> salt

Heat ½ to ⅝ inch of oil in a skillet on high heat; the oil should almost cover the fillets. Salt each piece of bass, and then shake it in a bag of cormmeal. Put 3 or 4 pieces into the skillet, then reduce the heat to medium high. Each setup will be different and will change as you cook, requiring constant adjustment. Watch your skillet carefully. When the bass browns on the bottom, turn the pieces with tongs (never a fork), and brown the other side. Do not cover the skillet. Drain the fish on 2 brown grocery bags, one atop the other. Serve hot.

Deep-Fried Sesame Bass

Sesame oil, as used in China, is made from browned sesame seeds and has a slightly burnt taste. It is good for seasoning but is a little too strong (and far too expensive in American markets) to use as a frying medium. Small amounts can be used for flavor, usually in a marinade.

> 2 pounds bass fillets
> ½ to ¾ cup sesame seeds
> 1 tablespoon sesame oil
> 1 tablespoon soy sauce
> 1 or 2 beaten chicken eggs
> flour
> salt and pepper
> peanut oil for deep frying

Mix sesame oil, soy sauce, salt, and pepper. Put the fish into a nonmetallic bowl, pour the mixture over them, toss to coat all sides, and marinate for 30 minutes. Heat the oil in a deep fryer to 375 degrees. Put some flour into a bag and shake the fish in it. Dip each piece in the beaten egg, then roll it in sesame seeds. Deep-fry several pieces at a time until golden brown. The fish is done when it floats. Drain on a brown bag, and serve while hot.

Bea's Cajun Fry

I know many people who sprinkle a few drops of Tabasco sauce over fish fillets and "marinate" them for a couple of hours before frying. I like the resulting taste, but I sometimes prefer another method. It doesn't require marinating and can be used in camp or for a quick shore lunch. I'm naming this recipe for a cook named Bea, from New Orleans, who used it to fry Sacramento River catfish for M. F. K. Fisher.

pan-dressed or filleted bass
2 cups stone-ground fine white cornmeal
2 tablespoons cayenne pepper
oil
salt

Mix the cornmeal and cayenne. Heat the oil for frying. Salt the bass pieces, and shake them in the cornmeal. Fry in hot grease until browned on both sides. Do not overcook. Drain well, and serve hot.

Note: You may want to test the cornmeal and cayenne mixture before frying the whole batch of bass. Mix as directed above, then salt and flour a small piece of the fish, fry, and taste. Add more cayenne or more flour, depending on your tastes.

Mustard Bass

Although I usually fry bass and similar fish with a coating of stone-ground cornmeal, here's a recipe I like to use from time to time—especially when I've got homemade mustard. Ordinary yellow mustard will do, but try brown Creole or fancy French mustard if you've got it.

bass fillets
prepared mustard
all-purpose flour
salt and pepper
cooking oil

Salt and pepper the fillets. Shake them in a bag of flour. Spread some mustard on a plate, and roll the floured fillets in it. Shake again in the flour. Fry in hot oil until golden brown. I like to use a deep fryer with this recipe, but a skillet will also work. If you do use a skillet, watch that the bottom of the fillets don't burn.

Big Batch Fried Bass

I got the idea for this dish from a recipe by Mrs. J. T. McCabe of Columbia, South Carolina, as printed in *The South Carolina Wildlife Cookbook*. The frying instructions and batter are of interest, but what I want to emphasize here is the method of draining the fish. If you have a large batch of fish to fry, the problem is keeping the ones on the bottom warm but not soggy with grease. Two thicknesses of brown grocery bags will help, up to a point.

> bass fillets
> cornmeal
> prepared mustard
> Worcestershire sauce
> thinly sliced rings from large onions
> green onions, chopped with part of green tops
> salt and pepper

Rig for deep frying at 375 degrees, and put down 2 or 3 large brown grocery bags on your draining tray or area. Sprinkle a batch of bass fillets on both sides with salt and pepper. Dip the fillets in a mixture of mustard and Worcestershire sauce (about half and half). Then shake the fillets in a small bag with a little cornmeal. Quickly put them in the hot grease, and cook until they are golden brown. The fillets are done when they float to the top, but I like to cook the thicker pieces another half a minute or so. I take the fish out with tongs, picking the brownest pieces as I go. Place the fillets in a layer on the brown bags. Prepare another batch, and put them in the fryer. While this batch is cooking, place a layer of onion rings and chopped green onions atop the cooked bass. When the second batch is done, drain some of the grease, then put them on top of the first batch. Repeat the layers until all the fish have been cooked. Of course, the onions can be eaten along with the fish. It's a great way to serve. If you want to get really fancy, add a few sprigs of fresh parsley and maybe some sliced lemon on top of the pile.

Variation: Instead of Worcestershire sauce mixed with the mustard, try wine vinegar. Or yogurt.

12

Kosher Fried Bass

Here's a recipe I've adapted from *The Jewish Festival Cookbook,* which said it originated with the Jews of Portugal. The dish is served cold with dill pickles, olives, and mayonnaise for the late Sabbath afternoon meal. The original recipe calls for haddock or other preferred fish. I use bass fillets. Note that the recipe calls for coating the fish first with matzo meal or flour and then with beaten egg, instead of the other way around. Try it.

>   3 to 4 pounds fish fillets
>   matzo meal or flour
>   2 or 3 chicken eggs
>   water
>   quartered onions
>   oil
>   kosher salt (or sea salt) and pepper

Sprinkle the bass fillets with salt, cover them, and put them into the refrigerator for several hours. Rinse the fillets, pat them dry, and sprinkle with pepper. Spread matzo meal or flour on a sheet of waxed paper. Whisk the eggs, thinning them with a little water. Heat ½ inch of oil in a skillet, and sauté the onions until they are golden brown. Drain. Coat each piece of fish with matzo meal, dip into the beaten egg, then quickly fry in hot oil. Do not overcrowd. Brown the fish on both sides, then drain on absorbent paper. Serve cold, along with dill pickles, olives, and mayonnaise.

Note: Sprinkling the fish with salt and letting them sit for a long period draws some of the moisture out of the fish and changes the texture, so that the fried bass will be quite different. It's a good technique to use with fish that tend to be soft, such as crappie, but remember that removing some of the moisture makes it very important not to overcook the fish.

Sautéed Bass

This recipe is a good one to cook in camp because it doesn't require lots of oil to be toted in. A little butter will do. If you are camping overnight, try cooking the recipe with bacon drippings left over from breakfast.

> small bass, dressed whole
> butter
> lemon juice
> flour
> salt and pepper

Dress the fish whole. Behead them if they are too long to fit into your skillet. Sprinkle the fish inside and out with lemon juice, salt, and pepper. Wait 15 minutes, then heat the butter in a skillet. Dredge the fish in flour, then sauté them on medium heat until they flake easily when tested with a fork. Don't serve these with the usual hush puppies and french fries. Try French bread, boiled new potatoes, and string beans. If you are so inclined, make a sauce or gravy with the skillet liquid by stirring in a little flour-and-water paste. Serve the gravy over the potatoes.

Jim Lee's Sweet-and-Sour Bass

A fellow from Tennessee tells me that the best fish he ever ate was in the Chinatown district of New York City. He didn't know the recipe, but the fish was fried whole and served with a sweet-and-sour sauce. I have tried such a recipe from Jim Lee, a native of China who settled in Manhattan, taught school, lived in a house converted from a matzo factory, and wrote about Chinese food. Lee was fond of what he called sea bass, and his description of the fish could well fit a black bass of average size. In any case, I use black bass with great success.

The fish, about 1½ pounds before it is dressed, is cooked whole in a deep fryer. The patio and camp fish cookers, especially those that are oblong in shape, are ideal for this purpose, but the little cylindrical kitchen counter deep fryers won't work if you want to cook the fish whole. I can cook a bass or two in a fryer designed for use on my stove-top grilling unit, but the gas-powered patio fryers with oblong frying pans are better. It is necessary to have lots of oil in the container—at least enough to float the fish. Heat it to at least 375 degrees.

The bass should be about 1½ pounds (before dressing) and no more than 2 pounds. I usually remove the head, tail, and fins. Don't snip off the fins; instead, cut down both sides of each fin with a small knife and pull out the fins and the associated bones that extend into the flesh. This is very important with bass. Preparing the fish in this manner makes it easier to eat with chopsticks or with a fork and spoon. The idea is to pull the meat from the backbone a bite at a time, then turn the fish and work on the other side.

> 1 or 2 bass
> 2 carrots, sliced
> ½ green bell pepper, sliced
> ½ red bell pepper, sliced
> 3 green onions, chopped with part of tops
> 2 slices canned pineapple
> ½ cup chicken stock
> ½ cup vinegar
> ½ cup sugar
> ½ cup flour
> 1 tablespoon cornstarch
> peanut oil (about 1 gallon for a large deep fryer)
> salt and pepper

Rig for deep frying. While the oil is heating, cut the pineapple slices into wedges. In a saucepan, mix the carrots, green onions, pineapple, sugar, vinegar, chicken stock, and a little salt. (Hold the peppers until later.) Bring the mixture to a boil, reduce heat to low, and simmer for 15 minutes.

Dry the dressed fish with a paper towel. Score the fish three times diagonally on each side. Sprinkle inside and out with salt and pepper, then roll the fish in flour to coat both sides. Put the fish very carefully into the hot oil, and fry until nicely browned on both sides. Carefully remove the fish, and drain on brown paper.

Heat the sauce almost to a boil. Add the peppers and cornstarch, stirring and cooking for 1 minute. Put the fish on a serving dish, pour the sauce over the fish, and serve. The Chinese put the fish on a platter in the middle of the table and eat it with chopsticks. If you want to make individual servings for each plate, cook a 1-pound bass (undressed weight) for each person. If you are eating téte-à-tête at a small table, however, do try putting a larger fish in the middle. It's more fun that way. In either case, be sure to serve the fish hot.

Cy Littlebee's Hush Puppies

Many people use onions and baking powder and wheat flour and other ingredients in their hush puppies. Here's an interesting recipe of this sort that was published by the Missouri Department of Conservation in the January 1953 issue of *Conservationist.* Note that Cy Littlebee says to roll the hush puppy into the shape of your thumb—a shape that may explain how the bread got the name "hush puppy" in the first place. Most folks think the name came about because a camp cook threw a piece of fried cornbread to a whining dog, saying, "Hush, puppy!" Maybe. Maybe not. The theory is too pat to suit me. According to a book on word origins, the people of the southern Ozarks used to eat fried water dogs, or mud puppies, a type of salamander, along with their cornbread and fried fish. But such fare was not considered to be a fit topic for polite table talk, and the fried water dogs were referred to, humorously, as "hush puppies." I have written about this theory at some length in another context, but apparently the world has little noted the derivation. Apparently some people don't want to know the truth. Whenever I start expounding the water dog connection and praising the culinary qualities of aquatic salamanders to our dinner guests, my wife always shakes her head, frowns, and says, "Hush, A. D."

16

2 cups cornmeal
1 cup flour
1 large sweet onion, finely chopped
4 tablespoons ham or bacon drippings
2 teaspoons baking powder
½ teaspoon salt
water

Mix all of the ingredients, adding enough water to make a fairly stiff dough. Form the mixture into elongated pieces about the size of your thumb. Fry the pieces along with the fish until the hush puppies are golden brown. These work better in a deep fryer.

Red Holland's Fried Corn Bread

A local television character by the name of Red Holland does a very popular early morning wake-up and fishing report, as well as the Saturday afternoon *Outdoors with Red* show for WTVY in Dothan, Alabama. Interestingly, Red is located a hundred miles away at Panama City, Florida, where he enjoys both fresh- and saltwater fishing. One morning, he made an unusual corn bread and said that he was sending a copy of the videotape to Ann Varnum, who does a good-morning show that often features local celebrity chefs, explaining that his tape would teach all those womenfolks up around Dothan how to make good corn bread.

Red was raised on Hoover's meal, made in Bonifay, Florida, and he still says that Hoover's is the best in the world. I don't know about that. Adam's meal, made in Midland City, Alabama, and Hall's, made in Columbia, Alabama, are both hard to beat. Other cooks in other necks of the woods will champion their own favorites.

Anyhow, Red specifies Hoover's meal and I'll allow it. The recipe is very short—and is exactly what I use in mine, as discussed in the recipe that follows Red's. The main difference between the two breads is in texture and shape.

Hoover's fine-ground white cornmeal
peanut oil
salt
water

Put some meal into a bowl and add a little salt. Stir in enough water to make a rather thick mush. Heat about ⅝ inch of oil in a skillet. Using your hands, shape the meal into patties, and then poke a hole in the center of each patty. Put the patties into the skillet—do not overcrowd—and fry until crisp on both sides. Drain them on brown paper. An obvious advantage of Red's method is that you get more crunch with a doughnut-shaped patty.

A. D.'s Skillet-Fried Bread

I confess that I never measure out the ingredients for my corn bread. Yet, it comes out exactly the same time after time. (Oddly, it *wouldn't* come out the same if I merely measured everything precisely and refused to adjust. Cornmeal, like wheat flour, varies slightly from batch to batch and maybe with the weather and the phase of the moon.) I start by mixing white cornmeal in hot water and a little peanut oil (or bacon drippings) until I have a mush that will drop nicely from a large spoon, making a piece about the size of a chicken egg. After stirring in a little salt, I let the mixture sit while I heat about ⅝ inch of peanut oil in a skillet—a cast-iron skillet, of course. Then I stir the batter again, and more often than not, I add a little more water, as the batter tends to stiffen as it sits. Next I spoon a little batter into the hot peanut oil. If the mixture is just right, the spoonful will flatten slightly as it settles on the bottom of the skillet. Proceed until the pan is almost full of bread. Cook on both sides over medium heat, turning once. When done, the outside of the hush puppy should be golden and crunchy; the inside should be mushy but hot. When the pieces are done to your liking, take them up with a spatula or tongs and let them drain on a brown bag. As they cool off a little, the insides will firm up considerably.

Although I don't measure the ingredients, I realize that most readers will need some guidelines. The following mix will be about right for making enough corn bread to feed 4 people.

> 2 level cups fine white stone-ground cornmeal
> 1 tablespoon peanut oil or bacon drippings
> 1⅞ cups hot water
> salt

Remember that the mixture will vary slightly from one batch to another, partly because cornmeals differ. It's best to start with the measures above, then add meal to thicken or water to thin until the mixture comes out of the spoon just right and flattens slightly as it slides into the skillet. Before starting, pour some hot water into a small bowl; dip the spoon into it from time to time to keep the batter from sticking.

Good Ol' Boy Hush Puppies

Use any good recipe for hush puppies, but cut the water measure in half and make up the difference with beer. Usually, they are cooked on the patio with a gas-heated fish cooker. It's best to cook these hush puppies for a group, so that you'll get various opinions over which brand of beer is the best to use. Some people say that Mexican beer is better, and I knew one fellow who insisted on dark German beer. A few women, on the other hand, will prefer Coors Light, which, they say, makes a lighter hush puppy. Personally, I prefer to drink the beer, if it is fresh, instead of putting it into bread. Suit yourself.

Bammie

If you are tired of hush puppies and yearn for something different, try this recipe from Jamaica. You'll need 2 pounds of fresh cassava. Tropical or subtropical, this root is a staple food in the Caribbean and many parts of South America. In many parts of the world, it is just as important as the potato. Cassava can be purchased in some specialty stores, and more and more I see it in our supermarkets. Sometimes it is called *yuca,* or *yucca, root.*

Peel the cassava root like an orange, and grate it onto a piece of cheesecloth. Bring the four ends of the cloth together and twist, forcing out much of the juice from the grated pulp. In an 8-inch skillet, shape the cassava pulp into a cake about ⅝ inch thick. Cook this on the stove top until the cassava cake sets. Then carefully turn it and cook the other side for a minute or two. Carefully lift out the cake with a large spatula. Heat ⅛ inch of bacon drippings in the skillet. Put the cake back into the skillet, and fry it for a few minutes on either side, turning once.

Fries and Chips

In many parts of the world, fried potatoes are considered to be a part of a fish fry. I'm not offering recipes here; anybody who can fry good fish won't have any trouble with the potatoes. I do suggest that you make the usual french fries if you are cooking with a deep fryer. If you are using a skillet or griddle, consider slicing the potatoes about ¼ inch thick and frying them on both sides, turning once with a spatula. Drain them on a brown bag, and sprinkle with salt and Hungarian paprika.

Although culinary traditions die slowly, I suspect that in the future we will eat fried potatoes with fish less often. After all, fried fish, fried hush puppies, and fried potatoes may be more than a little bit too much for modern health-conscious eaters. Something has to go. I'll keep the fish and corn bread and substitute something else for the potatoes. Believe it or not, grits are commonly served with fried fish in rural Florida, but unfortunately most cooks around the country don't know how to prepare grits properly, and most people (including some critics) have never eaten the real thing. (Frankly, I seldom ask for grits in any restaurant even in the South, because most of the ones I have eaten in the past were gummy and as such were unfit for human consumption.) I am very fond of sliced tomatoes with fried fish, if the tomatoes are homegrown or vine ripened. Anyhow, my advice is to experiment with salads and side dishes to serve with fried fish. Try jicama, an interesting import from Mexico, and Jerusalem artichokes. These can be purchased in some supermarkets or can be raised in the home garden in some climates. Both are very good merely sliced and eaten raw.

TWO

Skillet and Griddle Bass

Most of the recipes for frying fish can be cooked in a skillet. Here are a few others that work best in a skillet or on a griddle. Although I prefer cast iron, other skillets will do provided they don't have to be heated too hot. A heavy-duty skillet is almost always better for cooking than a thin one, simply because it conducts heat more evenly, although the backpacker might have a different perspective. In principle, I like those no-stick skillets that are made of heavy metal and then coated with some sort of ceramic material. Trouble is, they tend to crack if they are heated very hot. I've never seen a Teflon-coated skillet that didn't peel, and I've had several skillets warp, including an expensive one with a copper-coated bottom. Cast iron is inexpensive—and it lasts forever. I'm talking about American cast-iron skillets; some imports on the market are too light to suit me. I also try to avoid any skillet that doesn't have an ovenproof handle.

I like to have small, medium, and large skillets on hand. Most of my cooking is done in a 10½-inch skillet (measured across the bottom), but a 13-incher will hold twice as much and often comes in handy for cooking various recipes. I call these larger ones *jambalaya skillets*. I also like to have tight-fitting lids for the skillets, although I don't recommend lids for frying. Many cast-iron skillets are sold without lids, but they may be available separately. If your dealer doesn't have the lids in stock, ask if he can order one.

Black Bass with Green Peppers and Red Tomatoes, Cold

I cook this dish in a 13-inch cast-iron skillet with a lid. A large electric skillet will also work. If necessary, use a smaller skillet and sauté the fish in two batches, then combine everything for the final cooking.

> 2 pounds bass fillets or fingers (boneless)
> 2 large onions, sliced lengthwise into strips
> 2 green peppers, seeded and thinly sliced
> 2 large tomatoes, sliced
> ½ cup minced fresh parsley
> 4 cloves garlic, crushed
> 1 tablespoon tomato paste
> ½ cup olive oil
> salt and pepper

Pat the fillets dry, and sprinkle them with salt and pepper. Heat the olive oil in the skillet, and sauté the fillets, browning on both sides. Using a spatula, carefully move the fish to a brown paper bag to drain. Sauté the onions for about 5 minutes. Add the green peppers and sauté for another 5 minutes, stirring from time to time. Add the garlic, stirring for a minute or two. Add the tomatoes and parsley. Dissolve the tomato paste in a little water and add it to the skillet, along with a little salt and pepper. Add the fish, and spoon some sauce over the pieces. Cover the skillet and simmer (do not boil) for 15 minutes. Take the skillet off the heat. Carefully remove the fish to a serving platter, and top with the sauce. Chill. Serve cold with lots of good bread.

Bass Meunière

This famous recipe works fine with bass fillets. Essentially, it is fried or sautéed fish (usually coated with flour) topped with a sauce. The nice thing, from my point of view, is that the sauce is easily made in the skillet in which the fish was cooked.

2 pounds bass fillets, boneless
½ cup butter
flour
juice of 1 lemon
1 tablespoon chopped fresh parsley
salt and pepper

Heat the butter in a skillet. Sprinkle the fillets on both sides with salt and pepper, then dust with flour. Sauté the fish over medium heat until browned on both sides. Using a spatula, carefully remove the fish to a heated serving platter. Stir the lemon juice and parsley into the pan drippings. Then heat and stir for several minutes. Pour the sauce over the fish and serve.

Skillet Bass with Roux

You'll need a large skillet with a lid to cook this recipe, which calls for 2 bass of about 3 pounds each. A 13-inch cast-iron skillet will work, and so will a large, square-shaped electric skillet. If you want to cook more than 2 whole bass, or larger ones, try an oblong fish cooker designed for a camp stove. These can be used over two burners of a kitchen stove. When dressing the fish, I usually remove the head, tail, and fins, being careful to remove all the bones associated with the fins.

2 bass, whole (3 pounds each, dressed weight)
½ pound salt pork
2 cups chopped tomatoes
2 stalks celery with green tops, chopped
1 large onion, chopped
1 green pepper, chopped
4 tablespoons flour
salt and pepper to taste

Dice the salt pork, then sauté it in the skillet until the pieces are brown and crisp and most of the oil has fried out. Remove the pieces and save them. To the salt pork drippings, add the flour 1 tablespoon at a time to make a roux, stirring as you go. (You may have enough salt pork grease to absorb the flour. If not, add a little cooking oil, butter, or bacon drippings.) Stirring constantly with a wooden spoon, cook on very low heat until the flour is browned or until your arm gets tired—the longer the better, provided that the flour doesn't burn. Add the onions and cook for another 5 minutes. Stir in the tomatoes, green pepper, celery, and salt. Increase the heat to high. Place the fish in the skillet. Cover, decrease the heat to medium, and cook for 20 minutes without peeking. Turn the fish carefully, return the cover, and cook for another 10 minutes, or until the fish flakes easily when tested with a fork. The total cooking time for the fish will depend on the heat and the thickness of the fish, but the general rule is 10 minutes per inch of thickness. Carefully place the bass on a serving platter, and spoon the contents of the skillet over them.

Use the leftover pieces of salt pork to sprinkle over a tossed salad or over a baked potato with sour cream. Or nosh on them while you stir the roux and drink a beer or two.

Irish Creamed Bass

I don't know the history of this recipe, but I suspect that it is quite old. I adapted this version from a book of traditional Irish recipes, which called it creamed haddock, with a note saying that it would be suitable for cooking any white fish, such as cod. I find it to be a delicious way to serve bass fillets. It's very rich and filling, especially if you use real butter instead of margarine.

> 1 pound bass fillets, skinned
> 1 cup half and half
> ½ cup butter
> flour
> salt and pepper
> 1 teaspoon dry mustard
> fresh parsley

Skin the fillets, then sprinkle them with salt and pepper. Melt the butter in a small skillet or saucepan. Dip the fillets in the melted butter, then sprinkle them with flour. Place the fillets carefully in a large, well-greased skillet. Mix the half and half into the melted butter, then pour the mix over the fillets. Heat the skillet until the liquid around the fillets starts to bubble. Reduce the heat immediately, and simmer (do not boil) for about 10 minutes, or until the fish flakes easily when tested with a fork. (The exact time will depend on the thickness of the fillets and on the heat.) Carefully take up the fillets with a spatula, then gently arrange them on a heated serving platter.

Mix the mustard into the liquid left in the large skillet. Heat until it starts to bubble, then reduce the heat and simmer until the sauce starts to thicken. Pour the sauce over the fish. Garnish with parsley and serve hot. I like this dish with new Irish potatoes, English peas or snap beans, and canned pear halves stuffed with homemade mayonnaise and sprinkled with shredded cheddar cheese. If you're on a diet, however, you really ought to count the calories in all this.

Mexican Bass

This old Mexican recipe is for sea bass fillets, but it works nicely with black bass of medium size. The measures call for 3 pounds of fillets. That's about 7 or 8 pounds of undressed bass. If you cook this recipe from whole fish, be sure to save the backbones and heads for a stew or for a flaked bass recipe (see chapter 7).

> 3 pounds bass fillets
> 3 medium tomatoes, chopped
> 5 Mexican green husk tomatoes (tomatillos), chopped
> 1 medium to large onion, chopped
> 3 cloves garlic, minced
> 2 or 3 serrano chilies, seeded and chopped
> ¼ cup chopped fresh cilantro
> ½ cup peanut oil
> masa harina
> salt and pepper to taste

Remove the seeds and pith from the peppers. Wash your hands. Chop the peppers. Wash your hands again. Chop the tomatoes, green tomatoes, onions, garlic, and cilantro. Heat the oil in a skillet and warm a serving platter. Sprinkle the bass fillets on both sides with salt and pepper, then dust with *masa harina.* Fry the fillets in the skillet until they are nicely browned. (Don't crowd them in the skillet; cook in two or more batches if necessary.) Place the fillets on the warmed serving platter. Sauté the onions and garlic in the skillet for 5 or 6 minutes, adding more oil if needed. Add the cilantro, tomatoes, green tomatoes, salt, and pepper. Cook over medium heat, stirring constantly, until you have a thick sauce. Pour the sauce over the fillets and serve at once.

Note: If your produce market doesn't have fresh Mexican green tomatoes and chilies, substitute canned. Also, you can substitute parsley for cilantro. If you grow your own cilantro, or buy where the roots are included in the bunch, chop up some of the roots along with the leaves.

Serbian Bass

I don't know how ethnically authentic they are, but I've seen several recipes for Serbian carp. American black bass works just as well—or better.

> 2 pounds bass fillets (skinless)
> ¼ pound butter or margarine
> ¼ pound sliced mushrooms
> 1 medium onion, finely chopped
> 3 tablespoons tomato paste
> salt and red pepper (cayenne) to taste
> flour
> water

Heat the butter or margarine in a large skillet. Sprinkle the fillets with salt and very lightly with red pepper, then shake them in a bag with some flour. Sauté the fillets for 2 minutes on each side, then carefully place them on a brown bag. Sauté the onions and mushrooms for 5 minutes. Stir in the tomato paste, along with a little water. Put the bass fillets back into the skillet and simmer for several minutes. When fully done, the fish flakes easily when tested with a fork.

Vietnamese-Style Bass

All of the peoples of Southeast Asia love fish, and fish sauce (called *nuoc mam* in Vietnam) is commonly used in cooking and as a table sauce. This sauce is available in ethnic markets and in some American supermarkets, as well as by mail. (Also see the information on fish sauce in chapter 11, under Catsup and Other Bottled Sauces.) This wonderful recipe, *ca xao chua,* adapted from *Flavors of Southeast Asia,* makes use of the fish sauce in both ways. I cook the dish in a skillet large enough to accommodate 1 pound of boneless bass fillets. These fillets are in four pieces, so fillets from 2 bass of about 1½ pounds each are just right.

> 1 pound bass fillets
> 4 medium tomatoes, chopped
> 3 shallots, thinly sliced
> fish sauce, or *nuoc mam* (used two or three times)
> flour paste (see instructions below)
> 3 tablespoons peanut oil (used in two parts)
> black pepper
> 2 teaspoons white vinegar
> ½ cup water

Mix 1 tablespoon flour and 3 tablespoons water to make a paste, and set aside. Heat 1 tablespoon of peanut oil in the skillet, then lightly brown the fish fillets on both sides. Carefully remove the fillets and put them on a brown bag, then sprinkle both sides of each fillet with fish sauce, using a total of about 1 tablespoon. (This sauce is usually packaged in bottles with shaker tops. I estimate the measures.) Put 2 more tablespoons of peanut oil into the skillet, then sauté the shallots for 5 minutes. Add the tomatoes,

2 tablespoons fish sauce, and ½ cup water. Simmer for about 15 minutes. Add the flour paste, and stir until the sauce thickens. Carefully place the fillets back into the skillet and simmer for 3 or 4 minutes. Stir in the vinegar, being careful not to break up the fillets. Transfer to a serving dish. Grind a little black pepper over each fillet and serve. Like most fish dishes of Southeast Asia, *ca xao chua* is served with rice, and a bottle of fish sauce is usually put on the table for those who want it.

Note: You can also make this dish in a wok if you prefer. Since bass fillets flake easily, however, I prefer a large, flat skillet that doesn't crowd them up too much.

Blackened Bass

Fillets from 1-pound bass are ideal for blackening, a recent Cajun technique that became popular during the 1980s. To blacken properly, you need a cast-iron skillet or griddle (I prefer to use an oval fajita skillet for blackening), a hot fire, and a well-ventilated area, as well as some asbestos gloves with which to hold the skillet handle. The blackening technique is not recommended for the kitchen stove because too much smoke is created. Also, it is difficult to heat a skillet hot enough on many charcoal grills. Wood coals are hotter, and that's what should be used.

The method calls for hot spices, and commercial mixes are available in supermarkets and by mail order. Most of these come from Louisiana. Since I want a thick coat of spices on my fillets so that a crust will be formed, I find the premixed spices too hot. I usually use half blackening mix and half mild Hungarian paprika. There are some recipes for mixing your own spices, but most of these have a list of ingredients as long as your leg. If you like blackened fish that much, check out some modern Cajun cookbooks at your local library. I recommend that you start with the mixes because they are easier and cheaper in the short run.

After you heat the skillet, it's best to blacken one fillet at a time. Start by dipping the fillet in melted butter. (Do not put the butter into the hot skillet; it will go up in smoke.) Let the fillet drain for a few seconds, then flop it in a blackening spice mixture, coating both sides. Using tongs, grip the fillet by the small end and lay it onto the hot skillet. Count to 4, then turn the fillet with the tongs. Count to 3, and remove the fillet. If your skillet is hot enough, the surface will be crusted and the fillet will be done. (If in doubt, break one open in the thickest part; if the meat is opaque, it's done.)

Larger fillets won't work properly by the method above. The fillet must be about ½ inch thick, so that it will end up crusty on the outside and succulent on the inside. Although the technique is very easy, once you get the skillet hot enough, it must be an exact method in order to work. I might add, however, that some other books don't give the same advice and some restaurants seem to highly season ordinary sautéed fish fillets and call them blackened.

Always serve blackened fish with some cool salad and fire-quenching beverage. In season, try serving it with a generous pile of ice-cold watermelon cubes.

Griddle Bass

Another dish that I like to cook with an oval griddle isn't really a recipe—it's more of a technique. First sprinkle bass fillets with salt and pepper, then sauté them in a little melted butter, turning once. Remove the fillets with a spatula and place them on a heated serving platter. Add a little lemon juice and chopped parsley to the pan drippings, and sprinkle on a little flour. Stir and heat for a few minutes, then pour the pan gravy over the fillets. There are endless variations on this technique.

THREE

Poached and Steamed Bass

Although the black bass has a mild white flesh that lends itself well to the French poaching techniques and sauces, I feel that most Americans don't have the time and patience to pursue this kind of cooking. Most of the recipes below are self-contained so that you won't have to hopscotch all over the book in order to cook them. I do, however, cover some sauces and poaching liquids in chapter 11. In the French Bass recipe below, I describe the basic poaching technique and equipment.

The Chinese aren't quite as fussy as the French, but their cuisine does tend to be complicated for one reason or another. They do poach quite a bit, but steamed fish seems to be their forte. The reason, I think, is that steaming tends to leave the fish intact, whereas poaching tends to break it apart, especially if it is boiled in roiling water. The texture of some steamed fish, such as whole carp and bass, is firm but flaky, so that chunks can be pulled off nicely with chopsticks. Black bass is the perfect fish for the Chinese methods of cooking and eating, as in the following recipe.

There are several rigs for steaming whole fish. A bamboo steamer will work if the diameter is large enough to accommodate the length of the fish. Also, one of the long French poaching vessels can be rigged for steaming, provided that it has a tight lid and a suitable rack to keep the fish above the water level. (Usually, only a small amount of water is necessary for steaming.) I use a deep-frying rig designed to fit atop my stove-top grill. In any case, it is necessary to have the fish above the water level. Various sorts of racks can be used to elevate the fish. I prefer to put the fish on a serving platter and put the platter itself onto a rack above the water. This method makes it unnecessary to handle the fish after it has been steamed.

The steamed fish can be flaked and used in any recipe that calls for fish flakes (see chapter 7). Fillets can be steamed and served with a sauce, or the fish can be steamed and served whole. Whole bass in the 1- to 2-pound range work nicely. If you want to eat Chinese, cook a 2-pound fish whole and serve it on a platter in the center of the table, from which everyone eats with chopsticks. After the top side is cleaned to the bone, carefully turn the fish and work on the other side. The recipe for Chinese steamed bass calls for Chinese ingredients and is a good one to try by this method. If you can't wield the chopsticks, pull the meat off with two forks or a fork and a spoon, one in either hand.

I like to leave the head and tail on the bass, but I remove the fins by cutting along both sides of them with a small, sharp knife and then lifting them out. Be sure that you get all the bones. Any spine that sticks up will have a corresponding bone that sticks down into the meat.

French Bass

The French have long pans for poaching large fish; these usually fit across two stove burners or on a stove-top grill. Their long, slim shape allows the fish to be immersed in the liquid without requiring a large volume. These pans have tight lids and a rack with handles on either end, which makes it easy to take the fish out of the poaching liquid without tearing it apart. I have never owned such a pan, although I've always wanted one. Usually I have to rig for poaching in some other way. My stove-top deep fryer, for example, will handle a good-size bass. I have also poached in large outdoor fish fryers and in baking pans placed across two stove burners. A rack with handles is nice; you can rig such a rack by attaching cotton strings to the four corners of a flat rack of some sort. Or you can wrap the fish in wide cheesecloth, leaving the long ends sticking out. Twist the ends and you have lifting handles.

Although slightly salted water can be used for poaching, the French chef will insist on having a court bouillon, made as directed in chapter 11. A sauce is also required.

 1 whole bass, preferably with the head on
 court bouillon to cover the fish
 sauce

 Estimate the thickness of the fish at its thickest part. Put the fish into the poaching pan to make sure that it fits. Cover it with water, then pour out this water and measure it to determine how much court bouillon you'll need. (The slimmer the pan, the less liquid you'll need, which is, of course, the advantage of the French poaching gear.) Measure out the court bouillon, put it into a stock pot, and bring to a rolling boil. Now pour the court bouillon into the poaching pan, which should be over two stove burners or some source of heat, and turn on the heat. Bring to a simmer, cover, and turn the heat very low. The point is to poach, not boil. Set the timer; you want to poach the fish for 10 minutes per inch of thickness. To make sure it is done, see whether it flakes easily when tested with a fork. If perchance it's not done, turn up the heat and poach for a few more minutes. Do not overcook. Carefully remove the fish, and serve hot with the sauce of your choice.

Note: The liquid in the pan makes a good broth, which can be eaten hot with French bread. Or you can use it as the base for a soup. It's really too good to throw away. If you have leftover poached fish, flake up the meat and put it into a suitable measure of the broth, add a little parsley, black pepper, salt, and perhaps a little cream or half and half or a thickening paste made with flour and water. Heat for 10 minutes but do not boil. Serve in soup bowls with French bread.

Chinese Steamed Bass

Hoisin sauce and sesame oil are available in the Chinese section of most modern supermarkets and in ethnic markets. Sesame oil is made from toasted seeds and has a unique flavor. The salt-cured beans are a little harder to find, but they are usually inexpensive and worth the effort. They are called *dau she* in Chinese and are usually sold by the pound in plastic bags. I have also seen small packages at much higher prices.

> whole bass, about 2 pounds
> 2 green onions with tops, chopped
> 2 tablespoons soy sauce
> 2 tablespoons hoisin sauce
> 2 tablespoons peanut oil
> ¼ teaspoon sesame oil
> 1 tablespoon shredded ginger root
> 1 tablespoon salt-cured beans (optional)

Rig for steaming, but do not heat the water at this point. Dress the fish, leaving the skin on. Leave the head on if your steamer is long enough to accommodate it. Slash the fish diagonally across the body three times on each side. Wash and crush the salt-cured beans, and mix them with the soy sauce and hoisin sauce. Rub some of this mixture on the surface inside the bass cavity. Put the fish onto a platter of suitable size. Pour the rest of the sauce mixture over the fish, then sprinkle on the chopped green onions and shredded ginger root. Place the platter into the cold steamer and turn the heat to high. (You don't need much water in the steamer; it will quickly come to a rolling boil.) After the water boils, reduce the heat a little, cover the container tightly, and steam for 20 to 25 minutes, depending on the size of the fish. Bass over 2 pounds will require a longer steaming period; allow 10 minutes per inch of thickness plus 5 more minutes overall.

While the fish steams, mix and heat the peanut and sesame oils in a small saucepan for a couple of minutes. The oil should be hot but not to the smoking point. When the fish is done, pour the oil over it from one end to the other and serve. The skin of the fish is usually pulled off at the table.

The last time I cooked this dish, I had a 3-pound bass that was fat with roe. I rolled the roe in the soy sauce mix, then tucked it loosely inside the fish along with a sprinkling of chopped onions and shredded ginger root. It was delicious.

Note: This recipe has been adapted from Jim Lee's *Chinese Cook Book.* I have left out the monosodium glutamate. If you want it, add ½ teaspoon to the sauce mix.

Bass in Coconut Sauce

The island countries of Southeast Asia have an interesting native cuisine that depends on local ingredients and spices. Here's a dish that calls for coconut milk, which is not the juice inside the coconut, but a milky liquid obtained from the white meat of the coconut. (See the notes on coconut milk in chapter 11.)

> 2 pounds bass fillets
> 1 cup thick coconut milk
> juice of 1 lemon
> ½ teaspoon curry powder
> 1 medium onion, thinly sliced
> cinnamon stick, 2 inches long
> ½ teaspoon turmeric
> butter
> 1 tablespoon masa harina (or extrafine cornmeal)
> 2 cups water
> salt and pepper
> rice (cooked separately)

Heat 2 cups of water in a skillet with a tight lid. Sprinkle the bass fillets with lemon juice, then salt and pepper. Place the fish fillets in the skillet, cover tightly, and simmer for 10 minutes. (If your fillets are thicker than 1 inch at the widest part, increase the simmering time by 10 minutes per inch.) Carefully remove the fish and place them onto a heated serving platter. Save 1 cup of the liquid for use as stock.

Quickly heat the butter in a small frying pan or saucepan, and sauté the onion slices for 5 minutes. Add the retained fish stock, cinnamon stick, curry, and turmeric. Simmer for 10 minutes. Stir in the coconut milk and *masa harina;* heat it until it thickens, stirring as you go. Pour the coconut sauce over the fish, and serve hot with rice.

Easy Poached Bass

Don't tell the French, but one of my favorite recipes for poached fish is easy to prepare and doesn't require elaborate court bouillon or sauces. The clam juice can be purchased in cans in most supermarkets. Although I have listed 2 pounds of fillets in the ingredients, you don't have to use that much. It's best to have a pan wide enough to accommodate all the fillets at one time without overlapping. A large electric skillet is perfect.

2 pounds bass fillets, skinned
1 cup clam juice
1 tablespoon butter
1 shallot, minced
¼ teaspoon minced fresh basil
salt and pepper to taste

Heat the clam juice in a small saucepan, then mix in the basil, salt, and pepper; simmer for a minute, then turn off the heat. Heat the butter in a wide pan or electric skillet, then sauté the minced shallot for a couple of minutes. Flip-flop the fillets in the butter. Pour in the clam juice, increase the heat to high, bring to a simmer, reduce heat, cover, and poach for 5 to 10 minutes, depending on the thickness of the fillets. Test for doneness with a fork. Do not overcook. Remove the fillets with a spatula, and place them directly onto dinner plates. Spoon some of the pan liquor over each serving. Eat with French bread, salad, and vegetables.

Danish Bass Balls

Small poached balls of fish are called *quenelles* in French cookery, and recipes abound. Here's a good one from Denmark, usually made with fresh cod. Bass works perfectly.

> 1 pound bass fillets, skinless
> 2 cups milk
> 2 chicken eggs
> ½ cup potato flour
> ⅓ cup butter
> salt and white pepper

Cut the fillets into chunks, and run them through a meat grinder. Stir in the butter, flour, salt, and white pepper, mixing well. Run this mixture through the meat grinder 8 times. Put the mixture into an electric blender. On low speed, gradually mix in the milk. Beat the eggs and mix them in with the blender. Bring some water to boil, adding a little salt. With the aid of a spoon, shape the fish mixture into little balls, not over 1 inch in diameter, and drop them into the boiling water. Cook for about 10 minutes. Drain. Serve the bass balls topped with a sauce of your choice (I like the mushroom sauce in chapter 11) or drop them into a suitable soup.

Bass Salad

Here's a dish that I enjoy for a light lunch during the hot days of summer. It works best with chunks of bass rather than flakes.

> bass fillets
> hard-boiled chicken eggs
> lettuce
> mayonnaise
> herb vinegar
> salt

Poach the bass fillets for a few minutes in slightly salted water. When the fish are done, carefully remove them from the liquid with a spatula and break them into chunks. Put these into a nonmetallic bowl, and pour a little herb vinegar over them. Marinate in the refrigerator for 2 hours. Drain and serve over crisp lettuce leaves, topped with mayonnaise (homemade is best), and accompanied by hard-boiled eggs sliced in half lengthwise and some crackers.

Bass Veronique

Here's an easy but elegant dish that is accompanied nicely by a white wine, asparagus or other vegetables, and French bread. It works best with skinless fillets from a 12-inch bass.

2 pounds bass fillets, skinned
5 or 6 green onions
½ to 1 cup seedless grapes
½ cup fish broth (see chapter 11)
¼ cup white wine
salt and pepper to taste
mild Hungarian paprika

Mince the green onions with about half of the green tops. In a large skillet, heat the fish broth until it boils. Add the wine. Add the fish fillets, cover, reduce heat, and simmer for 5 minutes. Add the grapes, onions, salt, and pepper. Simmer for 5 minutes, or until the fillets flake easily when tested with a fork. Carefully remove the fillets with a spatula, and arrange them on a heated serving platter; put the grapes in the middle. Increase the heat under the skillet, and simmer the liquid until it is reduced by half. Pour the liquid over the fillets and grapes. Sprinkle the dish with mild paprika, and send to the table.

Gefilte Bass

Some sticklers for tradition might insist that this dish be made by stuffing a fish skin, which is difficult unless you are dealing with eel. Others say that it must be made with at least two—preferably three—kinds of fish. Most people these days prepare round balls or oblong pieces, instead of actually stuffing fish skin. Having several kinds of fish isn't really necessary, and the lean, white flesh of bass is quite satisfactory.

The Broth
6 cups water
1 carrot, sliced
1 medium onion, diced
1 tablespoon salt
1 teaspoon pepper

In a stock pot, mix all the broth ingredients, bring to a boil, cover, reduce heat, and simmer for 30 minutes. While waiting, prepare the following.

The Fish
2 pounds bass fillets, skinned
1 carrot, sliced
1 onion, chopped
2 medium chicken eggs
2 tablespoons matzo meal
2 tablespoons ice water
salt and pepper to taste

Run the fish, carrot, and onion through a food mill twice. Place the mixture into a food processor or blender, adding eggs, matzo meal, ice water, salt, and pepper. Mix at high speed until the mixture is fluffy. (If you have a food processor, use it for both operations.) Shape the mixture into balls or oblong pieces about the size of a tennis ball, and place into the hot broth. Simmer for 20 minutes. Carefully remove the balls and drain. Serve either hot or cold. This dish is often accompanied by horseradish.

Steamed Bass Tamales

Instead of starting from scratch with my favorite technique for making tamales, I have adapted this recipe from my *Wild Turkey Cookbook*. The basic technique is the same for both fowl and fish, although the filling will be a little different.

In addition to making a convenient wrap, corn shucks add flavor to food. Fresh corn shucks can be used, or dried shucks can be boiled or steamed for a while before using. (I prefer to simmer them in broth.) If you don't have your own, dried shucks are available in the Mexican food section of most supermarkets. If you prepare your own, it's best to square off the ends so that all the shucks are the same size. For the measures below, you'll need about 25 pieces of normal size.

Although this recipe can be made from leftover bass, I highly recommend that you start from scratch. You'll need a 2-pound bass, or 2 or 3 smaller ones. Fillet the bass and dice the flesh into small cubes; I use a chef's knife for this purpose. If you have time, put the fillets into the freezer until they are partly frozen; this will make them easier to cut. In any case, dice 2 cups of the bass. Save the head, bones, fins, and what's left of the fillets for the broth.

The Broth
head, backbones, fins, and any extra pieces of fillets
water to cover
1 medium onion, chopped
salt and pepper
1 bay leaf
¼ cup chopped celery tops or cilantro

Put the fish scraps into a pot of suitable size, cover with water, and add the other ingredients. Bring to a boil, cover tightly, reduce heat, and simmer for 1 hour. Strain out the bay leaf and other solids. Pull all the meat from the bones and head, add it to what's left of the fillets, flake it, mash it up, and put it back into the broth.

40

If you are working with dry corn shucks, add them to the broth, bring to a boil, remove from heat, and soak for 2 hours.

The Mesa
2 cups fine-ground cornmeal or masa harina
2 tablespoons shortening
1 teaspoon salt
fish broth (from above)

Before starting, measure out ¼ cup of broth and reserve for the filling; also remove the corn shucks, letting them drain. In a bowl, mix the fine cornmeal, shortening, and salt with enough broth to form a soft dough. Add hot water if you run out of broth. Let the dough stand for about 15 minutes, then add a little more hot broth or water if needed.

The Filling
2 cups chopped bass
1 tablespoon chili powder
1 medium onion, minced
2 cloves garlic, minced
1 teaspoon salt
⅛ teaspoon cayenne pepper
¼ cup fish broth (from above)

Spread out the chopped fish. Mix the cayenne pepper, salt, and chili powder, then sprinkle this mixture over the fish. Mix in the onion, garlic, and broth.

Spread out a few of the corn shucks on a flat surface and spread a tablespoon of mesa in the center of each. Over the mesa, spread a tablespoon of the fish mixture. Roll the shucks, then tie off the ends neatly with cotton twine. (Some people fold over the ends, but I prefer the twine to make the tamales hold together better.) When all of the tamales have been wrapped, rig for steaming.

A bamboo steamer works fine if you have one, or you can make a steamer by putting a rack in the bottom of a large pot.

Then stand the tamales on end. If you have a two-burner oblong pan of some sort, rig a rack on the bottom and place the tamales on it lengthwise. I often use a deep fryer designed to fit atop a stove-top grilling unit. In a pinch, improvise a rack from carrots, celery stalks, venison ribs, or other bones. When you have rigged a suitable rack, pour in the broth before loading the tamales. Bring to a boil, cover tightly, reduce heat, and simmer for about 45 minutes, or until the shuck and tamale dough separate easily.

If you're in a cooking mood, double or triple the measures above. Then freeze the tamales for later use. A couple of minutes in a microwave heats them up just right. Leave the shucks on during the freezing, but if you plan to keep them very long, it may be a good idea to wrap them again in plastic film. Use aluminum foil only if you plan to heat them in a regular oven.

Bonus eating: If you have leftover broth, try it as a soup. If it is too rich for you, add some canned stewed tomatoes (or Rotel, a mixture of tomatoes and chili peppers) along with the juice from the can.

Yankee Bass

I don't deny that finding three recipes for bass in *The Maine Way* came as something as a surprise to me, because I had been led to believe that most people in Maine don't care much for bass, saying that they taste muddy. But perhaps times are changing. Slowly. Two of the three recipes, however, were submitted to the Maine publication by Harry Moy of Cambridge, Massachusetts. One of these is for poached bass and calls for roasted peanuts, an ingredient that interested me because I was born and raised on a peanut farm. As printed in the Maine book, the recipe called for 1 scallion. I have changed this to 4 green onions. The recipe also called for 4 tablespoons vegetable oil. I have reduced this measure by half, specifying 2 tablespoons olive oil.

The fish is cooked whole, and I prefer to cook it with the head and tail intact, although the Maine book said to cut off the head and fins. Well, merely cutting off the fins leaves some bony spines in the top and bottom of the bass, and I recommend that you cut these out with a small blade. Note that the book said to scale the fish instead of skinning it, which indicates that not all Yankees recommend skinning a bass! Any sort of long pan that will hold the fish can be used, but it should have a lid. I have left roasted peanuts in the recipe lest I seem to be too fussy, but I really prefer to use peanuts that have been fried for a few minutes in peanut oil. Packaged peanuts can also be used. The original also called for salt to taste, but I find that the soy sauce is salty enough.

> 1 bass of about 2 pounds
> water for poaching
> ½ cup roasted shelled peanuts
> 4 green onions, chopped with half of green tops
> 3 tablespoons soy sauce
> 2 tablespoons olive oil
> 2 cloves garlic
> large mild onion (optional)

Place the fish in a suitable pan and cover it with water. Bring to a light boil, quickly reduce heat, cover, and simmer—do not boil—on very low heat until the fish flakes easily when tested with a fork. While poaching the fish, heat the olive oil in a small skillet and sauté the garlic cloves. When the fish is done, carefully place it on a serving platter, pour the soy sauce over it, then sprinkle with chopped green onions and peanuts. Discard the garlic, and pour the oil out of the skillet onto the fish. Top with thin slices from a large, mild onion, if you like onions. Serve hot.

Note: You can also poach small bass of about 1 pound for each person to be fed. The ingredients in the recipe will be enough for 2 small bass. Double everything for 4 small bass. The fish are easier to handle if you wrap them in cheesecloth, twisting the ends to serve as lifting handles. But the cheesecloth makes it more difficult to test the fish with a fork. The Maine book says that the fish is done when a toothpick can be pushed into it easily.

Variations: Add 1 tablespoon of chopped fresh parsley or chopped fresh watercress to the garlic.

FOUR

Baked Bass

When dressing a whole bass for baking, I recommend that you leave the skin on it. The skin will help hold in the moisture and, I think, makes a more attractive fish for the table. But some people, unfortunately, simply don't want skin on their fish and therefore won't think it is attractive. The chances are good that anyone who objects to the skin will also object to a whole fish on the table, in which case you should perhaps consider another method of cooking. If you do bake a skinned bass, try wrapping it in lettuce or collard leaves, or cook it inside aluminum foil or in a baking bag. It will be partly steamed instead of truly baked, but it will be more succulent.

Some of my favorite recipes for baked bass call for fillets instead of whole fish, and these are covered later in this chapter. Baked dishes with fish flakes are covered in chapter 7.

Baked Stuffed Bass

This recipe calls for a whole large bass, including the head and tail. I do, however, recommend that the fins be cut out carefully to remove the bones. (If you don't know how to do this, see step 4 of appendix A.) The cut removes the bones associated with the fins, making the fish much easier to eat, and helps the fish to cook through. The bass can be any size that you consider to be large—maybe 5 pounds and up. Allow 1 pound of undressed fish per person.

1 large bass
thin bacon
3 cups bread crumbs
½ cup butter or margarine
1 medium onion, chopped
1 rib celery with green tops, chopped
1 teaspoon thyme
salt and pepper
juice of 1 lemon
lemons for garnish

Dress the bass as directed above, leaving the skin on. Make three diagonal slashes on each side of the fish with a sharp knife. Roughly measure the thickness of the bass at the widest point. Preheat the oven to 400 degrees. Melt the butter in a skillet, and sauté the onions and celery for 5 minutes. Stir in the bread crumbs and thyme, along with a little salt and pepper. If the stuffing is too dry, add some of the butter from the pan to moisten it. Set aside.

Rub the fish inside and out with lemon juice, then sprinkle it inside and out with salt and pepper. Grease a suitable baking pan. Fill the bass's cavity loosely with the stuffing mixture, and close the opening. Wrap bacon around the bass's midsection, and secure it end to end with round toothpicks. The bacon will help keep the bass closed and the stuffing in. Then cut a piece of bacon in half and place it lengthwise along the fish's tail section. Place the fish in the baking pan, and put the pan in the center of the oven. Bake for 15 minutes, then reduce the heat to 350 degrees and bake for 10 minutes per inch of thickness.

Do not cook the fish too long. To determine whether it's done, test the fish at the thickest part with a fork before serving; when done, it will be opaque all the way to the backbone and will flake easily. If you don't trust your oven thermostat or your gut feeling about when a fish is done, it may be best to use a meat thermometer on a large fish. Insert the thermometer at an angle into the thickest part, just above the rib cage, but not deep enough to touch the backbone. Cook until the thermometer reads 140 to 145 degrees. No longer. Serve hot, along with lemon wedges.

Variations: There are endless variations on fish stuffings and seasonings. If you want to eat Italian, for example, sprinkle the bass inside and out with Italian spices (a blend is available in the spice section of supermarkets) and use Italian bread crumbs in the stuffing. Top the fish with thin slices of tomato and sprinkle with grated Parmesan. Then wrap it with thin bacon.

Cuban Black Bass or Red Snapper

Now that the threat of Communism seems to be on the wane, perhaps I can reveal that this recipe is from the old Cuba, where it was often used with red snapper as well as black bass, which grow fat and sassy in Lake Zapata and other good island fishing holes.

> 1 black bass or red snapper, 3 to 4 pounds
> 1 can tomato sauce (8-ounce size)
> 1½ cups shredded cheese (see below)
> salt and pepper

Preheat the oven to 350 degrees. Fillet the fish, and cut out the throat part. (This choice piece of meat is rather triangular in shape and has an odd bone structure; it is located between the pectoral fins and the gill plate.) Butter a baking dish that is just large enough to hold the fish. Sprinkle salt and pepper on both sides of the fillets and throat. Place the fillets into the dish, pointing in opposite directions, and fit in the throat. Pour the tomato sauce over the fish, spreading it around equally. Sprinkle the fish evenly with the shredded cheese. Put the fish into the center of the oven and bake for 20 to 25 minutes, or until the cheese browns nicely. (If it hasn't started browning after 20 minutes, turn the heat up to 450 degrees.) I normally use sharp cheddar because I like it, but other cheeses of moderate flavor can be used. A mixture of half Colby and half Monterey Jack lends color to the white flesh of black bass or red snapper.

Easy Baked Bass

Here's a recipe that is very good and quite easy to prepare. It is perfect for boneless fillets from bass of 3 or 4 pounds. Allow one such bass for 2 or 3 people. If you are a little short of meat, add the throats.

> bass fillets
> lemon juice
> mayonnaise
> salt and pepper

Preheat the oven to 450 degrees. Grease an oblong baking dish, preferably one suitable for serving. I like the oblong Corning Ware dishes. Squeeze lemon juice over the fillets, and sprinkle both sides with salt and pepper. Arrange the fillets in the baking dish in a single layer, skin side down. Cover each fillet with mayonnaise, spreading it on about ¼ inch thick. Bake for 10 minutes, or until the fish flakes easily when tested with a fork.

Easy Bass and Chips

Here's another easy dish that I like to make, especially when I've got leftover potato chips from a party or picnic. It can be cooked with fillets, but I usually use whole small bass.

> bass
> salted butter
> potato chips

Preheat the oven to 350 degrees. Crush the potato chips. Melt some butter in a skillet, and roll the bass in it. Then roll the bass in the potato chips. Arrange the bass in a greased baking dish, and drizzle some butter over them. Bake for 30 minutes in the center of the oven, or until the bass are nicely browned and flake easily when tested with a fork. The exact time will depend on the thickness of the fish and on your oven.

Variation: Try hot Cajun potato chips.

Tidewater Bass

Some of the best bass fishing I have ever enjoyed was in waters near the sea. I call those fish tidewater bass, for they can be caught, at times, in streams influenced by the tides or in the larger bays whose salt content has been diluted by large influxes of fresh water. Local hot spots can be found from Chesapeake Bay to Mexico. One of my favorites is the Apalachicola River in Florida, where fishing with large live shrimp in and around logjams sometimes provides fast action. In any case, tidewater bass are usually frisky. Feeding on needlefish and crabs and shrimp as well as the usual frogs and freshwater minnows, they grow fat and sassy.

I got the recipe below from the Outer Banks area of North Carolina, where bass grow in small ponds on the barrier islands as well as in Currituck Sound, which was at one time one of the premier bass waters in this country. The recipe calls for 1½ pounds of crabmeat, and I assume that the cook will want to catch his own crabs, boil them for a few minutes, and pick his own meat. Landlubbers can buy crabmeat if they've got the purse for it, or they can substitute the imitation crabmeat that is often seen in supermarkets these days. This is good stuff with plenty of color.

The measures below make a good batch, usually enough to feed 10 or 12 folks.

> 4 pounds bass fillets
> 1½ pounds cooked crabmeat
> 6 strips bacon
> 3 pounds potatoes, peeled and sliced
> 1 pound onions, peeled and sliced
> 2 pieces toast
> ½ cup mayonnaise
> 1 chicken egg, lightly beaten
> fresh parsley
> salt and black pepper

Preheat the oven to 400 degrees. Grease a baking pan of suitable size with a strip of bacon. Place the bass fillets in the bottom, skin side down, in two layers. Put a thin layer of about half the sliced potatoes and onions. Sprinkle on a little salt and pepper. Layer the rest of the sliced potatoes and onions. Sprinkle on a little more salt and pepper. Space the strips of bacon across the top, cover with aluminum foil, and cook for 30 minutes.

While waiting, boil the crabs, and pick out 1½ cups of meat. Mix with the mayonnaise, chicken egg, crumbled toast, salt, and pepper.

Remove the baking dish, and line the sides of the fish with the crabmeat. Stick in a few sprigs of fresh parsley. Cover again with foil. Put the dish back into the oven, lower the heat to 350 degrees, and cook for 15 minutes. Remove the aluminum foil and cook for another 15 minutes, or until the potatoes are done.

A. D.'s Cypress Pond Bass

I am fortunate enough to have, within casting distance of my bay window, a 2½-acre cypress pond full of crawfish and 4- to 5-pound largemouth bass. What more could one ask for? If you aren't so fortunate, remember that you can catch plenty of crawfish and bass in every state except Alaska.

Be warned that you'll need lots of crawfish to make a full cup of dressed meat, unless you've got the large, red swamp species of Louisiana (which are now being raised commercially in other states) or a Tasmanian freshwater crawfish, which can weight up to 8 pounds. It's best to boil or steam the crawfish for 2 or 3 minutes before peeling them. Don't cook too long. Using a breaking motion, detach the crawfish tail from the head. (With luck, you'll pull out some of the good fat with the tail.) Starting at the big end, carefully pull the crawfish tail. When you reach the end, hold the middle fin of the tail, twist it, and pull gently. If all goes according to plan, the gut will pull out with the tail. If not, you may choose to cut into the meat from the top and get the gut out. You'll have a more tasty stuffing if you include some head fat with the crawfish meat. If you don't have quite a cup of dressed crawfish tails, boil a fish head for about 20 minutes or so and flake off the meat from the throat, cheeks, and other parts; use as needed to make a full cup.

1 bass, 4 or 5 pounds
1 cup cooked and dressed crawfish tails
4 or 5 strips of bacon
2 cups soft bread crumbs
½ stalk celery, finely diced
1 medium onion (tennis-ball size), finely diced
¼ cup butter or margarine
salt and pepper

Scale the bass, gut it, and remove the fins. (Remove the head and tail if the fish is too long for your baking dish.) Preheat the oven to 500 degrees. Heat the butter or margarine in a skillet. Sauté the onion and celery for 5 minutes, then add the bread crumbs, salt, and pepper. Stir until the crumbs brown slightly. Stir in the crawfish tails. Stuff the fish with the crawfish mixture. To hold in the stuffing, wrap strips of bacon around the fish and pin with toothpicks. Also put half a strip of bacon lengthwise along the tail section of the bass. Grease an oblong baking dish with half a strip of bacon, and place the bass in it. Put the dish into the hot oven for 10 minutes. Reduce the heat to 350 degrees, and bake for 30 minutes, or until the bass flakes easily when tested with a fork.

If you have any crawfish stuffing left over, don't throw it out. While waiting for the bass to cook, add a chicken egg to the stuffing, make it into a patty, and sauté it in the skillet. If the patty doesn't hold together, scramble it.

Bass Fillets with Walnut Stuffing

The technique for this recipe is almost like that used in the previous recipe, except that the stuffing is different. Fillet the fish, then simmer the head and backbone and flake off the meat. The backbone is cooked in just a few minutes, but the head will take longer; remove the backbone and flake it while the head simmers.

> fillets from a 4- or 5-pound bass
> bass flakes from head and backbone
> 2 cups dry bread crumbs
> ½ cup walnut pieces
> ¼ cup chopped onion
> ¼ cup chopped celery with tops
> butter
> ½ teaspoon sage
> salt and pepper

Preheat the oven to 350 degrees. Melt 3 tablespoons of butter in a skillet, and sauté the onions and celery for 5 to 6 minutes. Pour this mixture over the bread crumbs, then stir in salt, pepper, sage, walnut pieces, and bass flakes. Salt and pepper the fillets, stuff them as in the preceding recipe, and place in a well-greased baking pan. Dot the top with butter, and pour a little water into the bottom of the pan. Bake for 30 minutes, or until the fish flakes easily when tested with a fork. Very carefully remove the stuffed fish and place it onto a serving platter. Garnish with slices of tomato, small boiled potatoes, green beans, and so on. Serve with a mustard sauce (chapter 11), if desired.

Variations: Use wild nuts instead of walnuts. Hickory nuts, wild pecans, or pine nuts can be used. If you have black walnuts, mix half-and-half with some other nut.

Jerry Lake Bass

One of my favorite fishing holes sat in the middle of an orange grove near Tampa, Florida. In time, a developer mapped out a subdivision on the slope and put in more than a hundred septic tanks. Before long, the lake was polluted. The last time I fished it, I made my first cast with a buzz bait just as the sun was coming up. The bait made soap bubbles on the surface of the water. But I have memories of catching a hundred bass during a single morning from Jerry Lake—and memories of eating them for dinner in the old Florida farmhouse that sat on its banks. In addition to 10,000 orange and grapefruit trees, the grove also contained a few old avocado trees, and I remember the fruits sitting on an open-air shelf on the screened porch of the old house, black and soft and nutty flavored.

3 to 4 pounds bass fillets
6 vine-ripened tomatoes, chopped
1 large very ripe avocado
1 medium onion, minced
3 cloves garlic, minced
juice of 2 lemons or limes
flour
½ cup olive oil
Tabasco sauce
salt and pepper

Preheat the oven to 325 degrees. Heat the olive oil in a skillet. Salt and pepper the fillets, and dust both sides with flour. Sauté the fillets for 2 or 3 minutes on each side, then place them in a greased baking dish that is large enough to hold the fillets without overlapping. Sauté the onion and garlic in the remaining olive oil in the skillet for 5 minutes. Add the chopped tomatoes, and stir for 3 minutes. Pour the skillet contents over the fish in the baking dish. Sprinkle with additional salt and pepper, cover, and bake for 20 minutes.

Meanwhile, scoop the avocado meat out of its rind and mash it with the lemon or lime juice, a drop or two of Tabasco sauce, salt, and pepper. Taste this mixture, and add more Tabasco or salt if needed.

Carefully remove the fillets with two spatulas and place them on a warmed serving platter. Quickly pour the tomato sauce out of the baking pan and into the skillet. Bring to a boil, and reduce the liquid by half. Stir the avocado sauce into the reduced tomato sauce. Pour the mixture over the fish, and serve. Feeds 6 to 8.

Greek Bass

I adapted this recipe from *The Frugal Gourmet Cooks Three Ancient Cuisines,* by Jeff Smith. Smith got it from Archestratus, a Greek from Syracuse, who reportedly wrote a cookbook in 330 B.C. I believe that only parts of the Archestratus text have been found, and apparently this recipe survived. Something of a snob, Archestratus said that the best fish come from Byzantium. Apparently he never ate a spotted bass from the upper Choctawhatchee.

> boneless fillets from large bass
> grape leaves
> green onions with tops
> white wine
> fresh lemon juice
> marjoram
> salt and pepper

Pay attention first to your grape leaves. If you have fresh leaves, soak them for a while in hot water. If you are using canned leaves, wash them in cold water. Note the size of the leaves, and cut your fish fillets into chunks that can be completely covered in a single leaf. (The fillets shouldn't be more than 1 inch thick.) Spread the leaves on a counter, and put a chunk of bass in each one. Sprinkle atop each piece of fish some chopped green onions, including part of the tops, along with a little marjoram, salt, pepper, and lemon juice. Wrap each chunk of fish in its leaf, tucking in the sides as you go, then carefully put it into a well-greased baking dish or pan of suitable size to hold all the fish. Sprinkle a little white wine over the leaves, and bake uncovered for 20 minutes in an oven preheated to 350 degrees.

Note: I have also read somewhere that fig leaves can be used instead of grape leaves. Tender wild grape leaves can also be used, but some of these are really too small to make a satisfactory wrap.

Yucatán-Style Bass

Many of the old Mexican recipes are for red snapper, grouper, and other good fish caught along that country's long coastline on the Pacific, the Gulf of Mexico, and the Caribbean. In recent years, new impoundments in the interior have been stocked with black bass and now offer some of the best fishing in the world. The old recipes work nicely with them, and many of the recipes can now be enjoyed in the United States because the ingredients are becoming available. Cilantro, for example, can be bought fresh in many of our supermarkets. The recipe below is from the Yucatán, where annatto seeds are used in cooking for flavor and color, much like saffron. They are available in Mexican, Indian, Spanish, and Caribbean food outlets and in spice stores.

This recipe, adapted from *The Complete Book of Mexican Cooking*, is one of my favorite ways for cooking medium-size bass whole. I scale the fish, remove the innards, and leave the head on.

> 1 medium bass, 5 or 6 pounds
> juice of 1 orange
> juice of 1 lemon
> 1 large onion, finely chopped
> ½ cup green olives, sliced
> ½ cup chopped fresh cilantro
> 1 can pimentos (4-ounce size), chopped, plus the juice
> ¼ cup olive oil
> 2 hard-boiled eggs, chopped
> 1 teaspoon ground annatto
> salt and pepper

Preheat the oven to 400 degrees. Sprinkle the bass with salt, pepper, and lemon juice. Place it in a long baking pan and set aside. Heat the olive oil in a skillet, then sauté the onion for about 5 minutes. Add the pimentos and the juice from the can, olives, annatto, and cilantro. Simmer for 3 or 4 minutes, then stir in the orange juice. Pour the sauce over the fish, and bake for 30 minutes, or until the fish flakes easily when tested with a fork. Garnish with chopped eggs and serve hot. Feeds 5 or 6.

Bass in a Bag

Bass cooked by this method are really steamed as well as baked. Modern plastic baking bags make the dish an easy one, although it may not be as quaint as bass cooked in parchment paper or brown bags.

2 pounds bass fillets, skinned
1 medium green bell pepper
1 medium red bell pepper
1 large onion
2 cloves garlic
¼ cup butter, melted
1 teaspoon salt
¼ teaspoon pepper
sweet paprika (optional)
plastic baking bag

Preheat the oven to 375 degrees. Peel the onion and slice it into rings. Remove the seeds and pith from the bell peppers, and slice them into rings. Peel and mince the garlic and mix with peppers and onions. Dip the fillets in the melted butter. Mix the salt and pepper, and sprinkle onto the buttered fillets, covering both sides. Place the plastic baking bag in the center of a baking pan and open it wide. Put the onions, peppers, and garlic in the bag, and spread them out, making a bed. Carefully place the fish fillets on top, and pour the remaining melted butter over the fish. Close the baking bag, and puncture holes in the top, following the manufacturer's directions. Bake for 20 minutes. (Fillets from larger fish, 4 pounds or over, will require an extra 5 minutes or so.) Remove the pan from the oven, slit open the top of the bag, and carefully transfer the fillets directly to individual plates. Sprinkle the fillets lightly with paprika, then arrange the onion and pepper rings around them. Serve with hot bread.

Bass au Gratin

An *au gratin* is an excellent dish for serving bass to people who think they don't like it. Use skinless, boneless fillets. It's a rich dish, so a little goes a long way. A pound of fillets will serve 4, if you've got plenty of vegetables, salad, and bread.

> 1 pound bass fillets
> 2 cups cream of mushroom soup
> ½ cup grated cheddar cheese
> ½ cup dry bread crumbs
> salt and pepper

Preheat the oven to 425 degrees. Poach the fillets in lightly salted water for 5 minutes, then place them in a greased casserole and sprinkle them with salt and pepper. In a saucepan, heat the soup, and add half of the cheddar cheese to it, stirring until the cheese is melted. Pour the sauce over the fish. Mix the rest of the cheese with ½ cup bread crumbs. Sprinkle the mixture over the fish. Bake in the center of the oven for 10 minutes, until the top is nicely browned.

FIVE

Grilled and
Broiled Bass

I'll try to be honest without laying all my cards on the table. (I might even keep an ace up my sleeve for a few paragraphs.) First, let me say that black bass is not ideal for either grilling or broiling. Both methods imply direct, intense heat and dry cooking. Since bass has lean flesh, it tends to become too dry when cooked by these methods. Second, bass is a flaky fish that tends to tear apart when it is turned or handled.

In both grilling and broiling (as I define them), the fish is cooked close to the source of heat for a short period of time. In broiling, the fish is under the heat. In grilling, the fish is over the heat, a process that provides a little smoke in addition to the heat. Broiling is usually accomplished in a kitchen stove; grilling, on a patio grill or campfire, using a rack over hot coals. But modern kitchen grilling equipment, either built into the stove or auxiliary indoor grills, is changing all this. These days, I probably grill more fish on my Jenn-Air electric range than on my patio grill. I'm not saying that I enjoy the indoor grill more. I'm simply saying that I tend to use it more often because it is so convenient.

The secret in either broiling or grilling is to cook the bass as close as possible to the source of heat (preferably an intense heat) so that the inside of the fish gets done while the outside gets nicely browned. This results in the quickest possible cooking time, which in turn results in a succulent, moist fish. (Fatty fish, such as lake trout or mackerel, can be cooked for a longer time on lower heat, and some of these fish might even profit by

57

letting some of the fat cook out; this is especially true when grilling fatty fish, in which case the drippings would cause some smoke to flavor the fish.)

For cooking bass, neither grilling nor broiling should be complicated by other methods of heat. It's simple radiant heat, whose intensity drops geometrically with the distance between the heat and the fish. Close the oven door or the lid of the grill, and you have convective heat to figure into the equation. Closing the lid of the outdoor grill might have other advantages as well, such as exposing the fish to more smoke.

Cooking the fish as close as possible to a high heat for a short period of time leaves it succulent, whereas cooking it farther from the heat tends to dry it out. For this reason, thin fillets or small fish are better for true grilling or broiling than thicker pieces. With the larger pieces, you'll have to increase the distance from the heat to the fish, and you may also have to close the lid of the grill or even use some sort of indirect heat scheme in order to get the fish done on the inside without burning the outside. This can be done successfully, and might even be turned to your advantage if you have some good wood smoke in the grill, but the fish simply won't be grilled or broiled, in my opinion.

Since the bass doesn't have much oil in the flesh, basting with a little oil or butter will help—up to a point. With quick grilling, however, the main purpose of the baste is to keep the surface in good shape and to add some flavor. A little oil on the surface also helps the fish hold a little salt and pepper and perhaps other seasoning. Basting too often, however, will interfere with the cooking. Again, let me say that basting won't work magic, and the best way to get succulent bass is to grill or broil the fish precisely and impeccably.

The other problem is that the flesh of bass is flaky and tends to tear apart during normal handling. Greasing the grill and the fish itself will help prevent the bass from sticking. I always grease the grill lightly before building the fire or turning on the heat, then again after it is hot. To turn a whole fish or fillet, work a spatula under the fish, coaxing it away from the grid if it has stuck. When the piece is loose, place a second spatula on top, and turn the fish. For better control, I recommend short-handled spatulas instead of those long ones that come in sets of barbecue tools. Also, the spatula should be thin and made of a springy steel. (A salesman down at the kitchenware section of my local hardware store seems to think I am a little picky in these matters.)

An adjustable grilling basket is the ace in the hole. I'm talking about a flat, rectangular basket; those fish-shaped baskets are usually not as practical. With a basket, you can turn the fish simply by turning the whole basket.

In both grilling and broiling, the cut of the fish is important. Since bass meat is flaky, it tends to tear apart when it is handled or turned, especially toward the end of the cooking process. Here are some guidelines for various cuts of bass.

Thin fillets. Fillets from small bass cook quickly and are ideal for broiling or grilling very close to the heat. You can broil them successfully without turning, but if you're grilling they must be turned over. A hinged basket is almost necessary. Grilling racks with small holes and a smooth surface have become available in recent years. These are good for thin fillets, not because they prevent sticking or tearing, but because the small grid keeps the pieces from falling through. I recommend that both thin and thick fillets be cooked with the skin on.

These fillets can also contain the rib cage, depending on how you dress the fish. Or you can cut out the rib cage if you want boneless fillets. You can also fillet the fish by cutting the flesh off the rib cage, but this flesh will be very thin and will tear easily.

Thick fillets. Large bass will result in thicker fillets. These can be grilled successfully but shouldn't be as close to the heat as thin fillets. It is tempting to grill the fillet whole, but it will be less likely to tear apart during handling if you cut it into sections.

Steaks. Steaks, usually cut from very large bass, grill nicely and marinate well. They are usually easier to turn than fillets. The texture is quite different—so different that your guests might not recognize a steak as flaky bass. It is difficult to cut steaks uniformly without having an electric saw, and I recommend that you take your lunker bass to your meat processor for steaking. The steaks should be a uniform thickness; I recommend 1 inch. I leave the skin on.

Butterflied Bass and Boned Bass. To butterfly a fish, remove the head and cut down the back as close as possible to the bones. Cut through the ribs, as when making a regular fillet. But don't cut through the belly. Remove the innards, then flop the fish open. If you want a boned bass, make a similar cut on the other side and remove the backbone. Fish that are hot-smoked by the indirect method are often boned, with the skin and scales left on. The fish is cooked without turning, and the flesh is simply pulled away from the skin with a fork (or your fingers) in convenient bite-size pieces. Bass can be treated in this manner, but the method is more suited to hot smoking than to direct grilling. Butterflied small bass, however, can be cooked under a broiler, in which case the fish is not turned. This method should be used for informal occasions, since the fish is sent to the table with the scales on.

Kabobs and Spitted Bass. Although fish are delicious when cooked on skewers, I consider the black bass, with its white, flaky flesh, to be unsuitable for this purpose, as well as for spitting and cooking on a rotisserie. On the other hand, modern grills come with all manner of attachments and baskets. If you can handle kabobs or spitted bass, have at it. Just keep the fish basted with butter or bacon drippings and sprinkle on a little lemon-pepper seasoning after each basting. Do not overcook.

In her short book *How to Cook a Wolf,* published in 1942, M. F. K. Fisher set forth some wise words about broiling and grilling fish. "A fish," she says, ". . . should be washed, dried, and then oiled, before it is seasoned for the grill. There should be plenty of melted butter, preferably heated with lime or lemon juice in it; and that, in most cases, is the perfect sauce, without even the distraction of a few minced herbs." Later, she added some notes to the original text, saying that she often rubs soy sauce on the fish before she oils it. Fisher also says, "If the fish is good at all, its flavor will emerge much more honestly if it be simply broiled rather than covered with an intricate and expensive sauce." At the risk of further irritating the French, who are already after me regarding my view on wines, I'll have to say that

I agree with Fisher completely. I would, however, recommend experimenting with onion juice, pomegranate juice, and so on instead of always sticking to lemon juice. But I insist that the juices be freshly squeezed, if possible.

GRILLING

Most of the recipes below will work on any grilling rack placed over a source of heat—electric, gas, charcoal, or wood. Let me emphasize that you don't really need recipes for grilling bass, and no marinade is required. Merely basting the fish a couple of times with melted, salted butter with a little lemon juice mixed in is about as good as you can do. But if you get tired of that simple method, here are some recipes to try.

Easy Patio Bass

Many of the good ol' boys in my neck of the woods grill fish with the aid of Italian dressing and a covered grill. Sometimes they marinate the fish for some time; other times they merely use the dressing as a basting sauce. Instead of basting with a brush, however, they simply shake up the bottle of dressing, partly cover the opening with the thumb, and pour some atop the fish in a small stream. This method will usually produce quite a bit of smoke, which is part of the ritual. It's best, I think, to use boneless bass fillets, but small bass can be grilled whole. In either case, grill over a wood coal or charcoal fire, placing the fish about 6 inches above the coals. Closing the lid will give the fish a little more smoke flavor and reduce flare-ups.

Grilled Bass Steaks

Here's a technique for cooking bass steaks on the grill. I like it because all of the steaks can be cut to the same thickness (preferably 1 inch), making the grilling time the same for all. Wrap each steak with a piece of thin bacon, and pin with a round toothpick. (Round toothpicks are thicker than the flat kind.) The bacon should not wrap more than once around the steak, overlapping just enough to hold.

Brush the surface of each steak with bacon drippings, then grill over a hot fire, on a greased rack about 4 inches above the heat. From time to time, baste the fillets with bacon grease and sprinkle lightly with lemon-pepper seasoning. The total grilling time should be about 10 minutes, but this can vary, depending on your fire and grill position as well as on the thickness of the fillets. Be warned that the bacon drippings can cause flare-ups, so grilling by this method is a full-time job. You will probably have to move the steaks about from time to time to avoid burning. I use tongs for this purpose, and I prefer to have a large grilling surface so that the steaks can be moved easily.

Marinated Bass Steaks

This recipe can be made with thick fillets, but I think it's best when made with bass steaks, as described in the previous recipe.

> 1 to 2 pounds bass steaks, 1 inch thick
> ½ cup olive oil
> ½ cup dry white wine
> 1 tablespoon white wine Worcestershire sauce
> 3 cloves garlic, crushed
> 1 tablespoon chopped fresh parsley
> salt and pepper
> Tabasco sauce (optional)

Put the fish into a nonmetallic container. Mix the rest of the ingredients (adding a few drops of Tabasco, if desired), and pour the mixture over the fish. Toss to coat all sides, and marinate for 30 minutes at room temperature or for 1 hour in the refrigerator. Preheat the broiler and adjust the rack so that the top of the fish will be 3 inches from the heat. Broil from 10 to 12 minutes, basting a time or two with some of the marinade. I think it is best to broil for a couple of minutes after the last basting, because the marinade contains uncooked fish juice, but some other books recommend basting with some of the marinade immediately before serving. Suit yourself.

Bass Hobo

Although it isn't really grilling, here's a wonderful way to cook a bass of about 1 pound or the fillet of a larger bass. It's best to cook a separate hobo for each person. The dish can be cooked on a patio grill, campfire, or kitchen grill.

> 1 small bass or fillet
> 1 medium potato, sliced
> 1 medium onion, sliced
> 2 slices bacon
> flour
> 2 teaspoons white wine Worcestershire sauce
> salt and pepper

Heat the grill. Dress a small bass with the head on, or use a fillet from a large bass. If using a whole bass, score it three times diagonally on each side. Place a sheet of heavy-duty aluminum foil on a flat surface, and put down one strip of bacon, lengthwise. Add a layer of potatoes and a layer of onions, using half of both. Sprinkle the bass inside and out with salt, pepper, and flour. Place the bass on the layer of vegetables. Put down a layer of onions and top with a layer of potatoes. Sprinkle with the white wine Worcestershire sauce and more salt and pepper. Put a second sheet of aluminum foil over the fish, and seal with the bottom sheet. It's best to make a fold at least 1 inch wide, and then make a second fold in the first; this will seal in the juices and steam. Place on the hot grill for 30 minutes, carefully turning once.

Serve with rice and salad, or serve as a complete meal. I like to sop the juices with hot French bread.

BROILING

Some chefs say that fish can be broiled without turning, but I have had problems with this advice in the past and I suspect that the no-turn advocates cook the fish too far from the heat, thereby losing some essential goodness of perfectly broiled fish, or else they use fillets of flounder, which are thin and flat. At a restaurant in Miami, I was once served a broiled fish that simply wasn't done except on the surface. It had not been turned. When I complained, the waiter took issue with me, as if it were impossible for their chef to send to the table a raw fish. But he took it back and brought another one. It too was raw on one side. I told the waiter to take the fish back and tell the chef to turn the fish over and cook both sides. Of course, he overcooked it on the next go-around.

Be warned that exact cooking times for impeccably broiled fish simply can't be given in any recipe. Too much depends on the source of the heat, the distance from the fish to heat, and the thickness of the fish. The expert can usually get it right, but most of us will want to flake a piece of the fish with a fork before sending it to the table. This is especially true of fish broiled with the backbone intact.

A. D.'s Griddle Broil

I don't really have a list of ingredients for this recipe. Essentially, it is for broiled fish basted with various combinations of butter, lemon juice, onion juice, and so on. The main idea is not the ingredients, but the technique.

I preheat the broiler, then I heat a greased griddle on the stove. Next, I put the fillets onto the hot griddle and cook for 1 minute. Then, quickly, I put the whole griddle under the broiler to finish cooking. The technique works best with fillets from ½ to ¾ inch thick. The advantage is that you don't have to turn or handle the fillets with a spatula.

If you want to try it, use a griddle with an ovenproof handle. I prefer the small, oblong fajita griddles. I use a separate griddle for each serving, and I serve the fish on the griddle resting on a wicker mat made for the purpose. The 2 fillets from a 1-pound bass fit nicely on the oval griddle. Try basting them with a mixture of butter and lemon juice, then sprinkling lightly with salt and pepper. Mushroom halves can be fitted around the fillets.

Onion Juice Bass

A good number of recipes for broiled fish call for a basting sauce made of butter and lemon juice. Here's a recipe to use when you don't happen to have any lemons on hand, or if you'd like to try something different.

> bass fillets
> mild onion
> butter
> salt and pepper

For each pound of bass fillets, squeeze out 2 teaspoons of onion juice. I do this by first chopping the onion and then crushing the pieces in a garlic press held over a bowl, catching the juice and throwing out the pulp. I do insist on having freshly squeezed juice; onion juice sold in bottles won't do. Melt ¼ cup of butter in a saucepan. Stir in the onion juice along with some salt and pepper. Baste the fillets well on both sides. Broil, basting once or twice while cooking. Do not overcook.

Black Bass Red Holland

I got wind of this recipe early one morning, before daybreak, when Red Holland's morning show came on the air. I had gone to sleep with the TV on, and Red woke me up. I dozed off again, waking up with a nagging memory of a recipe for broiling fish. But I couldn't remember the particulars. All I knew was that the recipe was short and sounded good. Later, I found a yellow stick-on note with the words *mayonnaise* and *soy sauce*. That was it!

Preheat the broiler to high. Mix equal parts of mayonnaise and soy sauce. Place the bass fillets on a greased rack about

4 inches from the heat. Baste thickly with the mixture, then sprinkle on a little salt and pepper. Broil until done.

Bass with Lemon Relish

The relish in this recipe goes nicely with bass fillets or other broiled fish. Here's what you need to make about 1 cup of relish, which will be enough for 2 pounds of bass fillets.

The Relish
½ cup sour cream or yogurt
¼ cup crushed pineapple, drained
1 tablespoon finely chopped green bell pepper
1 tablespoon finely chopped red bell pepper
1 tablespoon finely chopped onion
2 tablespoons diced peeled lemon
1 teaspoon grated lemon rind (zest only)
1 tablespoon light brown sugar
1 tablespoon dark rum
½ teaspoon dry mustard
½ teaspoon celery salt
¼ teaspoon ground allspice

Mix all the ingredients in a small nonmetallic bowl, and refrigerate until the fish are ready. Remember to grate only the yellow part of the lemon rind, avoiding the bitter white inner pith.

The Fish
2 pounds boneless bass fillets
butter
salt and pepper

Brush the fillets with butter, then sprinkle with salt and pepper. Broil close to the heat until done, turning once. Place the fillets directly onto plates, skin side down, and spoon a little of the relish over each serving.

Bass with Anchovy Butter

This recipe works best with boneless fillets. Any size bass will do if you adjust your broiling technique according to the general instructions set forth at the start of this chapter.

> bass fillets
> melted butter
> anchovy butter (chapter 11)
> lemon quarters or halves
> salt and pepper to taste

Preheat the broiler. Coat the fillets on both sides with melted butter, then sprinkle with salt and pepper. Broil for about 10 minutes (perhaps a little longer if you have fillets from very large bass), basting a couple of times with butter. Do not overcook. Carefully remove the bass to a heated serving platter or put directly on plates. Spread some anchovy butter over each serving, and garnish with lemon quarters or halves.

Variation: After you fillet your bass, poach the head and backbone until the meat flakes easily. Pull the meat from the bones with a fork, and break it apart. Stir some anchovy butter into the flaked bass. Then broil the fillets and spread the mixture over each serving.

Broiling Whole Fish

Broiling comparatively flat fillets usually works better than broiling whole bass. As stated elsewhere in this chapter, the ideal is to cook the fish quickly, coordinating everything so that the inside is done just when the outside is nicely browned. To accomplish this with whole fish, you have to lower the rack, increasing the distance between the fish and the heat. If you don't, the outside will burn before the inside gets done. Increasing the distance increases the cooking time drastically and tends to dry out the fish. Consequently, I don't generally recommend broiling whole fish.

But whole bass can be broiled successfully if you are careful. It's best to put them into a hinged basket or double grill so that turning won't be a problem. Slash each fish three times diagonally on each side. Rub the fish inside and out with bacon drippings or olive oil, then sprinkle with salt and pepper. Put the fish into a hinged basket, and cover the top side of the fish with thin strips of bacon or thin slices of lemon. Turn the basket, unhinge it, and cover the other side of the fish in the same way. Preheat the broiler. For 1-pound bass, place the rack 8 inches from the source of heat, and broil for about 10 minutes on each side. The fish should be done when the bacon looks ready to eat and the skin has started to separate along the top fins. If in doubt, test with a fork. Sprinkle with mild paprika and serve hot.

Greek Bass

Oregano is popular around the Mediterranean, especially in Greece, where a rather strong variety is cultivated. Although the herb is not usually associated with fish dishes, except perhaps for shrimp or crab, it can be used successfully with broiled fish. But remember that a little goes a long way with a mild fish such as black bass. If you are out of oregano, substitute marjoram.

> 2 pounds bass fillets
> ⅓ cup olive oil
> juice of 1 lemon
> ½ teaspoon oregano (or marjoram)
> salt

Mix the olive oil, lemon juice, and oregano in a small bowl and let sit for a few minutes so that the flavors will blend. Sprinkle the bass fillets lightly with salt. Preheat the broiler. Coat the fillets with the olive oil mixture, and broil for about 10 minutes, or until the fillets flake easily when tested with a fork, basting several times. Serve hot.

Wild Onion Bass

I first cooked this recipe after I caught a few small bass while wading beautiful Spring Creek in Georgia, a bridge or two above Lake Seminole. Here the water ran swift and crystal clear. As I walked up the bank to my car, I noticed thousands of wild onions growing on the embankment. I pulled up a handful, grabbing them by the green tops. If you can't find any wild onions, use green onions from your garden or the supermarket.

>   2 pounds fillets from small bass
>   ½ cup butter
>   juice of ½ lemon
>   ½ cup minced wild onions with half of tops
>   salt and pepper to taste

Heat the butter in a skillet, then sauté the minced onions for 5 minutes on low heat. Stir in the lemon juice, salt, and pepper. Preheat the broiler, and put the bass on a heated broiling pan or perhaps a skillet or griddle with a lip and an overproof handle. Place the bass 3 or 4 inches from the heat. Broil for 5 or 6 minutes, or until the flesh flakes easily when tested with a fork. (Larger fillets should be farther from the heat and cooked for a longer time.) Carefully remove the fillets to a heated serving platter, or serve directly on plates. Sprinkle on a little salt, then spread some of the sauce over each serving.

Note: Wild onions can be on the strong side. Add more butter if the basting sauce is too strong.

SIX

Smoked and Pickled Bass

Be warned that bass prepared by some of the recipes and techniques in this chapter aren't really cooked. Although I don't have a problem with eating raw bass if I have caught it myself and know that it is fresh, I feel that I should give my dinner guests and my readers fair warning. Some authors say that bass soaked in lime or lemon juice (as in the popular seviche), or salted down for a suitable period of time, is cooked. It isn't. Cooking requires heat. Other authorities say that freezing fresh small fish between 0 and 10 degrees for 24 hours, or large fish for up to 6 days, makes them safe to eat. Still, I prefer to catch and freeze my own bass.

I might add that some of the recipes below *are* cooked, and others can be used in cooked dishes. Casseroles and other dishes made with cold smoked fish are especially good. Fully cooked, hot-smoked bass is also covered in this chapter.

PICKLED BASS

Although *pickled* is sometimes used to refer to salted fish, the recipes and techniques below are for bass that have been more or less pickled with the aid of vinegar or lemon or lime juice. Raw fish, such as seviche, should be kept chilled before serving.

Bass Seviche

Fish that has been marinated for several hours in lemon or lime juice and then served raw is a popular appetizer in Mexico, Central America, and South America. Called *seviche,* it is usually served up with chopped tomatoes, onions, and green stuff. Use only very fresh fish, or fish that have been frozen while very fresh. Bass are ideal for seviche, at least for me, but some Latin Americans prefer fatter fish, such as mackerel.

Most good Mexican cookbooks have recipes for seviche, and there are many variations. This is one of my favorites.

1 pound skinless bass fillets
1 cup freshly squeezed lime juice
2 large tomatoes
1 medium white onion
½ yellow or green bell pepper, chopped
2 pickled serrano or jalapeño peppers
½ tablespoon minced fresh cilantro or parsley
2 tablespoons olive oil
salt and pepper

Skin the fillets, cut them into ½-inch cubes, put them into a nonmetallic bowl, and pour the lime juice over them. Refrigerate for half a day or overnight, stirring a time or two with a wooden or plastic spoon. When you are ready to proceed, remove the seeds and pith from the pickled peppers. Slice the onion and separate the slices into rings. To the chilled bowl of fish, add the onions, hot peppers, bell pepper, cilantro, olive oil, salt, and pepper. Peel the tomatoes, chop them, and stir them in.

Eat your seviche cold as a salad, appetizer, or light lunch. Good stuff.

Variations: Use lemons if you don't have a ready supply of limes, but remember that it really is necessary that the juice be freshly squeezed. Also, try thin strips of bass fillets instead of chunks. I have also made memorable seviche by soaking the fish overnight in lime juice, then mixing the fish with canned Rotel, a commercial mixture of chopped tomatoes and peppers. Chunky salsa will also work.

South Seas Seviche

In spite of its popularity in Mexico and South America, the basic seviche probably originated in Polynesia. Here's a recipe from Tahiti, which calls for coconut milk. Notice also that rice is used in this recipe (but not in the Mexican version), which brings to mind the Japanese sushi menus in which the raw fish is served on a bed of rice.

> 1 pound bass fillets, skinned
> juice of 5 large lemons or limes
> 2 tablespoons grated onion
> 1 cup coconut milk (see chapter 11)
> 1 teaspoon sea salt
> rice (cooked separately)

Cut the fish into ½-inch cubes and put into a nonmetallic bowl. Sprinkle with sea salt. Add the lemon juice and onion, stirring with a wooden spoon. Cover and refrigerate overnight. Stir with the wooden spoon from time to time. Drain the fish and add the coconut milk. Stir and refrigerate for 2 or 3 hours. Serve on a bed of rice in clam or scallop shells.

Variations: The fish can be sliced paper thin and marinated in lime juice for only 2 hours before serving. If you want something closer to Mexican seviche, omit the coconut milk and serve it in shells with chopped tomatoes and chopped green onions with part of the tops, along with a minced chili or two. Add a little cilantro and maybe some sliced jicama on the side. In Tahiti, sometimes chopped cucumbers and chopped hard-cooked chicken eggs are added to the dish.

Pickled Bass

I usually use this recipe for pickling suckers, pickerel, and other bony fish because the process softens the bones. But bass fillets work nicely, and I prefer that they be skinned and cut crosswise into strips about ½ to ¾ inch wide and 2 inches long. These bite-size pickles are easy to handle and sit nicely atop a cracker. The measurements in the recipe can be increased if you want lots of pickles. It's best to put them up in wide-mouth pint jars. Pickling spices are available in spice sections of most supermarkets, or you can mix your own from bay leaves, allspice berries, peppercorns, and cloves. Some people use the commercial Louisiana crab boil spices, packaged in convenient little bags.

> bass fillets
> 1 cup sea salt
> onions
> pickling spices
> wine vinegar
> water

Fillet freshly caught bass, and cut them into fingers as directed above. For each pound of bass, put 2 quarts of water into a nonmetallic container and dissolve 1 cup sea salt in it. (A Crock-Pot works nicely for this process.) Put the fish into the brine, and weight it down with a plate or saucer or a block of wood so that the brine completely covers it. Leave the bass in the brine in a cool place for 2 full days.

Rinse the fillets well in cold running water, and sterilize 2 1-pint jars for each pound of fillets. Put 1 tablespoon of pickling spices into the bottom of each pint jar. Cover the spices with thin slices of onion. (Or you can tie the spices in a piece of cheesecloth or use an old-fashioned tobacco sack if you have one.) Add a layer of bass fillets, then another slice of onion, repeating this process until the jar is almost full, ending with onions. Fill the jar with a mixture of half wine vinegar and half water. Cap the jar and refrigerate for 3 or 4 weeks before eating. The pickles will keep for several months.

Eat the pickles with saltines or use them in salads. I like them in "sling slang," mixed with canned sardines, canned oysters, chopped homegrown tomatoes, chopped mild white onions, black olives, Greek salad peppers, and so on, all served in a large wooden bowl and eaten with crackers and unrefrigerated hoop cheese. (Refrigerated cheese won't do.)

One-Step Pickled Bass

Here's an easy recipe that bypasses the brine soak. The measures below call for enough bass, cut into bite-size chunks, to fill a quart jar ¾ full. Adjust the measures if you've got more than 1 jar of bass.

skinless bass fillets cut into pieces
1 medium onion, diced
¼ cup sugar
3 tablespoons salt
1 tablespoon pickling spices
white vinegar

Fill a sterilized quart jar ¾ full of bass chunks. Add the diced onion, sugar, salt, and pickling spices. Then fill the jar almost to the top with white vinegar. Screw on the top, shake the jar, and refrigerate for 5 days. These pickles will keep in the refrigerator for 10 days, but they are best on day 7, I think.

SALT BASS

Before mechanical refrigeration was invented, salting was a way of preserving fish for long storage and was usually performed on very plentiful commercial fish, such as cod and herring. Salt fish is still available commercially, and some recipes for it are very good. I especially like some of the recipes from Africa and the Caribbean. If you like the flavor of salt fish, as I do, you may want to salt down a few bass from time to time.

There are two basic methods of salting fish: dry cure and brine. It's hard to go wrong with either method, provided that you apply enough salt for a long enough period of time. With stringent modern limits on black bass, there's no point in a long discourse on salting down large batches of these fish. If you want a few for your own table, the dry cure is probably the easiest way to go.

I recommend what I call the tilted plank method for salting down just a few fish. Scale and gut the bass, then cut them in half lengthwise. Salt both sides. Find a suitable length of unpainted board, preferably about 12 inches wide. Tilt the board slightly, fixing it so that the end will drain into a tray or some other container. The board should be in a cool place, preferably rather airy. (The last batch I prepared was in our air-conditioned laundry room, with the board tilted in a large sink.) Salt the board, and arrange the fillets on it, making sure that none of them overlap. Arrange them lengthwise, if possible, so that the water will drain off the board instead of from one fillet onto another. Cover the fillets with salt. Move the fillets around several times during the first 24 hours, turning and switching them about for proper drainage.

After 24 hours, take the fillets off the board and scrape off all the moist salt. Resalt the board, and put the fillets back on top, sprinkling them again with salt. Add more salt as needed. Let the fillets dry for several days. Then brush off the excess salt, and refrigerate or freeze the fillets until you are ready to eat them. Note that if you continue to put fresh salt onto the fillets, they will eventually become bone dry; such fish will be edible after a long soaking with water, but they won't be as good as lightly cured fish. In fact, the best salt fish might well be those that are caught late one afternoon, salted overnight, and rinsed and cooked for breakfast the next morning. Salt fish for breakfast might seem a bit heavy for modern readers, but it is a tradition in many parts of the world. My father was fond of eating salt mullet for breakfast.

Fried Salt Bass

Soak the salt bass for several hours in cold water to freshen it, preferably changing the water from time to time. Hard salt fish should be soaked overnight. Then dust the fish lightly in cornmeal or flour, and pan-fry it in hot grease. Most of the comments and recipes in chapter 1 can be applied to salt bass that have been properly freshened.

Salt Bass Patties

In parts of New England, patties made from salt cod are something of a tradition. Often the fish is mixed with mashed potatoes and fried. Here's my version.

2½ cups mashed potatoes, precooked
1½ cups flaked salt bass
1 chicken egg
2 tablespoons butter
pepper
oil for deep frying

Soak the salt bass for several hours in cold water, then poach it for a few minutes, or until the meat can be flaked easily. Rig for deep frying at 375 degrees. Mash together the potatoes, bass flakes, butter, and pepper. Beat the mixture until fluffy, then beat in the chicken egg. When the oil is hot, form fish balls and fry them until they are golden brown. It's best to drop the fish balls from a tablespoon, dipping the spoon into a glass of water from time to time so that the fish balls won't stick. I use two spoons, holding the ball until the last moment so that it won't splash hot oil. Drain the fried balls well on a brown bag, and serve hot.

Salt Bass Salad, Caribbean-Style

One of the world's great culinary ironies is that cod, a fish of northern climes, is a favorite in the West Indies and parts of the east coast of South America. In these places there is no shortage of good fish, such as the delicious flying fish and the dolphin (mahimahi.) Yet some of the best recipes for salt fish come from this area. Part of the explanation is that the early European settlers were not fishermen. They were plantation owners or developers (raising sugar cane and other products) and merchants. To feed the slaves, it was easier to buy salt cod from Europe, and the trade was encouraged by the various governments, merchants, and shipping interests. Another trade developed with New England shipping interests, hauling salt cod to the Islands and hauling molasses back to New England. The slaves—usually excellent cooks—developed some very good recipes using the salt cod, African cooking talent, and native American ingredients, such as tomatoes, avocados, and chili peppers.

There are thousands of these recipes from the Islands and from the eastern seaboard of South America, some of which have become traditional and are even served for breakfast. (Other good ones come from the West Coast of Africa.) This dish from Trinidad (where it is called *buljol*) is one of my favorites. It can be made with bass or any good salt fish as well as with cod. In fact, bass has a lean, white flesh that is similar to cod, although many of our older landlubbers might believe the cod to be oily because of the association with cod liver oil.

1 pound salt bass
4 medium ripe tomatoes, chopped
2 medium onions, chopped
1 ripe avocado
2 hot red peppers
juice of 2 lemons or limes
lettuce leaves
½ cup olive oil
salt and black pepper

Place the salt bass in a nonmetallic bowl, and cover it with boiling water. Cool and drain. Repeat the process. Drain the fish and press the water out of them. When the fish are thus freshened, remove the skin and bones, and break the flesh into bite-size pieces. Now prepare the vegetables. Many island chefs peel and seed the tomatoes, but this is not necessary. It is, however, necessary to seed the hot peppers and remove the inner pith before chopping them. (Wash your hands immediately after working with the hot peppers.) In a wooden bowl, toss the onions and tomatoes with the salt bass. Sprinkle with salt, pepper, olive oil, and lemon juice. Toss again. Serve on crisp lettuce leaves and garnish with slices of avocado. Well-to-do Island families usually eat this salad as a first course (or for breakfast), in which case it will serve 8 or more people. I prefer to have it as a light lunch or brunch, in which case the above measures feed 4 to 6.

Salt Bass Chowder

Salt bass works in most chowder recipes, especially those that call for potatoes. Here's a simple but good one from the Outer Banks of North Carolina, where potatoes are still called Irish potatoes.

> 1 pound salt bass fillets
> 4 large potatoes, diced
> 1 large onion, diced
> 1 teaspoon black pepper
> water

Put the diced potatoes and onions into a stove-top Dutch oven or other suitable pot, barely cover with water, and bring to a boil. Reduce heat, cover, and simmer for 20 minutes. Break the salt bass fillets into chunks and add them to the pot, along with the black pepper. Simmer for 15 minutes. Serve in bowls, and eat with plenty of hot bread.

Variations: If you want a thicker chowder, mix some milk or cream in with the water. Or mix in some fine stone-ground white cornmeal (if you can find it). I also like this dish made with red pepper flakes instead of black pepper; put the red pepper into the pot at the outset. You can also use a pod of dried hot pepper in the water, then discard it after cooking.

COLD-SMOKED BASS

Fish that are smoked at a temperature below 100 degrees F. are said to be cold-smoked. This process may or may not cure the fish, and fish must be treated in a salt brine to discourage bacterial growth. I also recommend that cold-smoked fish be cooked.

Cold smoking is easier to accomplish in cold weather; if the temperature outside is 95 degrees, it's going to be difficult to make smoke while keeping the temperature below 100 degrees. For this reason, the fire box and the smoking container are often separated for some distance with a flue or some sort of rigged conduit. The idea is to dissipate the heat before it reaches the fish. A thousand schemes for cold smoking have been devised, such as putting racks in a barrel and connecting it via a flue of some sort to a fire in a downhill box, so that the smoke will rise up to the fish. These rigs can be more or less permanent, or you can rig a temporary smoker at home or in camp. Even cardboard boxes can be fitted with racks and used successfully.

To cold-smoke, you must have enough heat to generate smoke—but not enough to cook the fish. Some of the commercial smokers use a hot plate to heat the wood, and you can rig your own from an electrical hot plate. Usually, a pan of some sort sits on an electrical heating element. The pan holds wood chips, shavings, or sawdust, which smolder and provide smoke without bursting into flame, thereby greatly increasing the temperature. Although I lean toward green wood, many people prefer sawdust because it gives off a dense smoke.

You can also get wonderful results by burning green wood slowly. Unless you have a very large smokehouse, a wood fire will have to be some distance from the fish.

Regardless of the rig, you'll need to soak the bass in a brine before smoking. Flavorings are often added to the brine, and there are many recipes. Here's one that I like.

A. D.'s Smoked Bass

Several bass, 1 pound each
1 gallon water
1 cup sea salt
5 cloves garlic, crushed
¼ cup white wine Worcestershire sauce
1 teaspoon Tabasco sauce

Scale and gut several bass of about 1 pound each or smaller. (Larger fish can be butterflied.) Put the fish into a nonmetallic container. Mix a brine with the water, sea salt, garlic, white wine Worcestershire sauce, and Tabasco sauce. Cover the fish with the brine, and weight it down with a plate or a block of wood or some other nonmetallic object. The fish must be completely submerged. Soak the fish for at least 12 hours. Drain the fish on a rack, and let it dry until a thin film forms. Place the fish in the smoker, and smoke for several hours. The exact smoking time isn't terribly important if you will use the fish within a day or two instead of curing it. Smoking the bass too long, however, makes it chewy. For long smoking, it's best to have a temperature well below 100 degrees.

Note: The sea salt used in this recipe has more minerals in it than common table salt, which has been refined. Some of these minerals are good preservatives, and others add flavor. You can now find sea salt in some large supermarkets, although it is more expensive than table salt.

Although I have eaten cold smoked bass just as it came out of the smoker, I recommend that you use it in recipes that require cooking. Here are a few to try.

Potatoes Stuffed with Smoked Bass

This recipe makes a good side dish to be served along with a complete meal. It is also good for brunch or lunch.

2 cups smoked bass flakes
3 large potatoes
1 medium onion, minced
2 tablespoons margarine
3 cloves garlic, minced
1 can cream of mushroom soup (10¾-ounce size)
1 cup grated Cheddar cheese
salt and pepper to taste

Bake the potatoes at 500 degrees for 45 minutes. Remove them from the oven, cut in half lengthwise, and spoon out the pulp, leaving a layer about ⅛ inch thick along the skin. In a skillet, heat the margarine and sauté the onions and garlic for a few minutes. Mash the potatoes and put them into a mixing bowl. Add the contents from the skillet. Mix in the mushroom soup, bass flakes, salt, and pepper. Reduce the oven heat to 400 degrees. Stuff the potato hulls with the fish mixture. Sprinkle the grated cheddar on top, dividing it more or less equally. Put the stuffed potatoes into the oven, and bake for 20 to 30 minutes, or until they are nicely browned on top.

Smoked Bass Casserole

Any good cold- or hot-smoked fish can be used for this casserole. Omit the salt from the recipe if the smoked fish has been heavily salt-cured before smoking.

2 cups smoked bass, flaked
3 medium potatoes
1 large onion
1 can cream of mushroom soup (10½-ounce size)
¾ cup grated cheddar cheese
salt, if needed
black pepper
margarine

Boil the potatoes for 20 minutes, then cool and slice them. While the potatoes are cooling, preheat the oven to 350 degrees. Slice the onion and sauté for a few minutes in a skillet, using a little margarine. Grease a casserole dish, and place alternating layers of potatoes, fish, and onion, in that order, starting and ending with potatoes. Sprinkle with salt if needed, and grind or sprinkle some black pepper on top. Spread the mushroom soup over the top, and sprinkle the cheese over the soup. Bake for 35 minutes, checking once or twice toward the end to see that the top doesn't burn.

Smoked Fish Patties

Here's one of my favorite dishes for smoked bass. It can also be made with leftovers from hot-smoked fish.

½ pound smoked bass, flaked
1 small to medium onion, chopped
1 cup cooked and mashed potatoes
1 chicken egg, beaten
½ cup cracker crumbs
2 tablespoons peanut oil
1 tablespoon chopped parsley or cilantro
½ tablespoon oriental fish sauce or Worcestershire
salt and pepper to taste

Crumble enough crackers to measure about ½ cup of crumbs, and flake enough smoked bass to make ½ pound of pure meat. Heat the oil in a skillet, and sauté the onions for about 5 minutes. Remove the onions, and mix in a bowl with all the other ingredients except the cracker crumbs. Shape the mixture into patties, then dredge them in the cracker crumbs. Turn the heat up to medium high, and fry the patties for a few minutes until browned on both sides, turning once.

HOT-SMOKED BASS

In hot smoking, the fish is flavored with smoke while it is cooking. This can be accomplished with a light smoke made by piling wood chips or shavings on or beside hot coals while grilling a small bass or fillet for only a few minutes, or a heavy smoke may be applied for half a day to a large fish. In either case, the fish is (or should be) fully cooked during the process.

The smoke used for this method is usually generated from store-bought wood chips or chunks, which should be soaked in water before being used. Although personal and regional favorites are hotly argued, any good hardwood or fruit tree will do. I will, however, argue that freshly cut green wood makes better smoke than dried wood soaked in water.

Silo Bass

The silo shaped smoker-cookers are very easy to use. Typically, these have upper and lower racks, a source of heat (charcoal, electric, or gas), a pan for wood chips, and a pan for water and drippings. If you follow the directions for your unit, it's really difficult to go far wrong with these rigs. Remember, however, that without water in the pan, you are essentially baking the fish, so cooking them too long will make them dry and chewy—in which case smoke won't help them very much.

A number of recipes call for wine and all manner of ingredients to be put into the water pan. It's my opinion that this is a very inefficient way to use wine. Cooks who promote the use of wine in stews say that the alcohol vaporizes and the flavor stays in the stew. If this is the case, the flavor stays in the water pan, does it not? (This may be an oversimplification on my part, but it's something to think about.) Further, the use of spices and other ingredients in the water pan is also suspect, in my view—especially when smoke is being used in the process. But suit yourself. If you do put ingredients into the water, try a couple of bay leaves for aroma.

I don't recommend these silo units for smoking large whole fish, unless you soak the fish in a brine cure for several hours to help retard bacterial growth. Fillets can be cooked without brine, as in the recipe below.

> bass fillets, boneless with skin
> bacon drippings
> salt
> water and wood chunks (or freshly cut wood)

If you are using dry wood chunks, soak them overnight in water before using. If you are using freshly cut green chips, which I recommend, no soaking is required. Coat the fillets with bacon drippings, then salt lightly on both sides. Heat the cooker, fill the water pan with water, and add the wood chips. Grease the rack and put down the bass fillets, skin side down, without overlapping them. Cover the unit, and cook for 1 hour. Then remove the hood and check the bass. It is important to test the fish from time to time so that it won't overcook—but remember that opening the hood too often cools down the unit drastically. Cooking times will vary, depending on your unit, the type of heat, the thickness of the fillets, and the outside temperature. Wind can also slow down the cooking process.

For fillets of medium bass, a total cooking time of about 2 hours will be about right. It's not necessary to keep up a good head of smoke, but water should be kept in the pan. Usually, a full pan will last long enough to cook fillets. It's OK to baste the fillets lightly with bacon drippings, if you do so quickly. The flavor of bacon drippings goes nicely with the smoke, but if you don't want the animal fat, you can substitute vegetable oil.

Grill-Smoked Bass

There are some excellent electric grills on the market, and most of these can be used for smoke-flavoring bass by simply laying a piece of hardwood (preferably freshly cut green wood) over the heating element. Most of these units are on the small side and are therefore more suitable for cooking fillets. Try basting the bass from time to time with butter and sprinkling lightly with lemon-pepper seasoning after each baste.

You can also use gas grills for smoke-flavoring fish. These usually work best for fillets of small fish, but the larger units can also be used for indirect grilling. Most of the larger grills have burners on either side, in which case the one opposite the bass can be used. Deluxe models may even have a special burner for indirect cooking. When grilling directly over heated lava rocks, a few dry herbs sprinkled over the fire will produce a burst of smoke.

You can also impart a smoke flavor to bass grilled over charcoal by adding wood chips to the fire.

Butterflied Bass

Butterflied fish are usually cut down the middle and left hinged by either the belly skin or the top of the back. The fish are not scaled and are cooked skin side down without turning. When done, they are served up on a plate or platter, or on a brown bag, with the scale side down. The flesh is pulled off in bite-size chunks with forks or with the fingers.

Bass of 2 or 3 pounds work best. Larger fish are difficult to get done in a reasonable length of time, and smaller ones are apt to cook too quickly to absorb much smoke flavor. Butterflied bass are usually cooked by the indirect method; that is, the fish is not placed directly over the hot coals. This can be accomplished with a circular grill, but it is best to use a large, rectangular grill with a hood or, better, a hinged barrel-shaped rig with a rack fitted inside. One of the best rigs I've seen was made from a 55-gallon drum split in half and hinged. Some of the larger commercial units available today have a large cylindrical section for smoking and an offset fire box. Ideally, the smoker-cooker should have a vent on one side so that smoke will flow across the fish. Using such a rig is easy, but the timing is difficult because of the infinite variations in outside temperature, heat of the fire, size of the grill, size of the fish, and so on. Experience is the best guide, but painstaking cooks can be successful on the first try.

Butterflied bass or fillets cooked with the scales on aren't normally marinated, but the flesh side is usually basted from time to time. Recipes for basting sauces are numerous, and you can hot-smoke a very tasty bass with only bacon drippings and a little salt. Again, technique is far more important than an exact basting recipe. Nevertheless, here's a recipe and method that you may want to try.

>whole bass, butterflied
>½ cup bacon drippings
>½ cup sake or vermouth
>½ cup soy sauce
>½ tablespoon brown sugar
>½ teaspoon black pepper

Build a good charcoal fire in one side of your covered grill, and let it burn down to coals. Add some soaked wood chips (or freshly cut wood pieces) around the edges of the coals. Grease the grid and the bass with bacon drippings. Place the butterflied bass on the opposite side of the grill, scales down. Ideally, the fish and the fire should be as far apart as possible. Close the lid, and adjust the vents so that you'll have a slow-burning fire. Mix the soy sauce, bacon drippings, pepper, and sake. Hold back ½ cup of this mixture and stir the brown sugar into it; this is a finishing sauce that will be used later. Baste the fish. Close the lid. Every 20 or 30 minutes or thereabouts, baste the fish and check on the fire, adding more coals or more wood as needed. When you do open the lid, attend to business quickly and get out. During the last 30 minutes or so of cooking, start basting with the brown sugar mixture.

Variations: If you've got some green wood on hand, cut a piece to fit crosswise into your grill. Place the charcoal fire next to the end of the grill, and bank it with the green log. You may also choose to use wood instead of charcoal; if so, be careful that your fire isn't too hot for long, slow cooking and smoking.

Hot-Smoking Lunker Bass

Large bass can also be smoked whole in the larger cookers by the indirect method. It's best to clean the fish, scale it, and soak it for several hours in a brine. (The brine will help prevent bacterial growth.) Then dry the fish, grease it, and proceed with indirect cooking and smoking as in the previous recipe. Use a baste of your choice. Plain butter or oil will do. If you want to leave the fish unattended for a while, drape some strips of bacon over it. (Using heavy-duty aluminum foil, you can rig a drip pan under the fish to catch the bacon drippings; this pan should go under the rack.)

Cooking a whole fish by this method is tricky, depending on your fire and the setup. If in doubt, use a meat thermometer inserted into the thickest part of the fish. The thermometer should not touch the backbone or rib cage. The fish is done when the thermometer reads from 140 to 145 degrees. In addition to assuring that your fish gets done, the thermometer can be a good aid in estimating cooking times and adjusting the heat level in the cooker. Most good cookers have a thermometer showing the internal temperature of the box, which can be adjusted by tending the fire or by opening or closing the vent, thereby regulating the oxygen to the fire.

SEVEN

Flaked and Leftover Bass

One day in the not-too-distant future, I predict, fish flakes and ground turkey will be as popular as hamburger meat is today. The best fish flakes are freshly made especially for a certain recipe. You can poach the fish for a few minutes, until it flakes easily when tested with a fork, or you can steam it for a few minutes. In either case, overcooking the fish will make it too mushy for a good flake. Poach or steam the bass no longer than 10 minutes per inch of thickness.

I often make fish flakes from bass heads and bony parts left from filleting. You can also use leftover fish for flakes.

Be warned that it takes a good-size bass to yield a full cup of flakes. As a rule, a 1-pound bass will flake out only about 1 cup of meat. In any case, the exact measure of the fish isn't critical for most of the recipes in this chapter, so you can go up or down ½ cup for recipes that call for 2 cups. You can also adjust the other ingredients if necessary.

Whatever method you use, be certain to get all the bones out of the fish flakes. Some of these recipes are so good that you tend to wolf them down without the usual caution, in which case you might swallow, or worse, partly swallow, a small bone.

Bass Casserole

There are thousands of casserole recipes that are suitable for leftover or flaked bass. Here's one of the best I've tried. It's tasty and attractive. The exact quantity of fish isn't critical, but I would prefer to have more than 1 pound rather than less. If you are using fresh fish, which I would highly recommend, figure on 2 pounds of undressed bass, then poach the fish and flake it. Get all the meat off the head and backbone.

> 1 pound bass flakes
> 1 medium onion, chopped
> 1 small bell pepper, chopped
> 1 stalk celery, chopped
> ½ cup chopped mushrooms
> 1 tablespoon chopped fresh parsley
> juice of 1 lemon
> 1 lemon, thinly sliced
> ½ cup cracker crumbs
> 1 chicken egg, beaten
> olive oil
> ¾ cup milk
> 2 tablespoons flour
> 1 teaspoon prepared mustard
> 1 teaspoon Worcestershire sauce
> salt and pepper to taste
> Tabasco sauce

Preheat the oven to 350 degrees. Heat 2 tablespoons olive oil in a skillet. Sauté the onion, bell pepper, mushrooms, and celery for 5 or 6 minutes. Stir in the flour, cooking for another 5 or 6 minutes. Slowly add the milk, stirring as you go, and simmer until the mixture thickens. Stir in the lemon juice, mustard, Worcestershire, 3 or 4 drops of Tabasco, and a little salt and pepper. Beat the chicken egg and stir it into the sauce. Stir in the parsley, then carefully stir in the bass flakes. Grease a casserole dish, and put the mixture into it, spreading it evenly. Put the cracker crumbs into a small bowl, and mix in a tablespoon of olive oil. Sprinkle the crumbs over the casserole. Place lemon slices over the casserole, and bake uncovered for 20 minutes, or until the top is nicely browned. Serve hot.

Easy Bass Sizzle

Heat a little butter in a skillet. Add bass flakes, salt, and pepper. Cook and stir with a wooden spoon until the fish starts to brown. Eat while hot.

As a variation, try a little minced onion, sautéed for 5 minutes before you add the bass flakes. In camp, use a small amount of wild onion, finely chopped watercress, or fresh (edible) mushrooms. Also, try garlic-flavored oil instead of butter.

Easy Bass and Chicken Eggs

One of the best ways to use up a small amount of leftover bass is to flake it and scramble with eggs for breakfast or brunch. Exact measures aren't necessary, within reason. It's easy to make up variations on this recipe, using whatever you've got on hand. This recipe is so good that you may find yourself cooking it with fresh bass, without waiting for leftovers—in which case it will be even better.

> bass flakes
> chicken eggs
> chopped green onions
> butter or margarine
> salt and pepper

Whisk the eggs in a bowl, and stir in the bass flakes. Sauté the chopped onions (with part of the tops) in butter for 5 minutes. Add the egg mixture, and scramble until the eggs are nicely set. Don't let them get too dry, however. Salt and pepper to taste.

Variations: Fry some bacon or salt pork in the skillet until crisp, set it aside to drain, and proceed with the pan drippings instead of butter. Serve the bacon along with the scrambled eggs and fish. If you've got a surplus of tomatoes in the garden, dice a mature green one and sauté it for a few minutes, then add the egg mix.

If you like the bass flakes and chicken eggs, be sure to try the next two recipes.

Sautéed Bass Patties

Most of the recipes for crab patties can be used for cooking bass flakes. Some of these burn easily, however, and should be fried or sautéed on medium heat instead of the high temperatures I recommended for frying in chapter 1. This dish is a good one to try with leftover or poached bass.

> 2 cups bass flakes
> 1 cup dry bread crumbs
> ½ cup milk
> 2 large chicken eggs, lightly beaten
> 2 tablespoons chopped fresh parsley
> 1 tablespoon white wine Worcestershire sauce
> salt and pepper to taste
> butter

Mix all of the ingredients except the butter, and shape into patties. Heat the butter in a skillet or on a griddle, and sauté the patties for several minutes, or until lightly browned on each side, turning once with a spatula.

Bass Patties with Fish Sauce

Although any good white-fleshed fish can be used for this recipe, I like to use small bass of about 1 pound each, which flake up just right. It's best to steam or poach the bass until it flakes easily with a fork, but leftover baked or even fried fish can also be used.

This recipe calls for Thai fish sauce, which can be found in oriental food stores. Happily, I can even purchase it off the shelf in a local supermarket. If you can't find the Thai sauce, substitute the Vietnamese fish sauce, which is similar but may be a little stronger. I suspect that both kinds are somewhat diluted for exportation to the United States. The ingredients list on the label of a commercial brand states, "anchovy fish extract, salt, sugar, and water." Traditionally, the fish sauce is made by packing small fish with salt in wooden barrels. What drips out is fish sauce. It may smell and taste a little strong to some people, but if you like it as much as I do, it's a wonderful ingredient for cooking and for use as a table sauce, and it is highly nutritious.

1½ to 2 cups bass flakes
4 chicken eggs, lightly whisked
2 green onions with half of tops, minced
2 tablespoons Thai fish sauce
1 tablespoon flour
¼ teaspoon black pepper
peanut oil

Steam or poach the fish, then flake off the meat with a fork. Spread the flaked meat out on a surface, and sprinkle the flour over it. Put the fish into a bowl. Stir in the whisked eggs, minced onion, fish sauce, and pepper. Heat a little peanut oil in a 9-inch skillet, then ladle or quickly spoon in about a quarter of the fish mixture (or simply pour it in from the mixing bowl). Cook the patty until the bottom is browned, then flip it over and brown the other side. Repeat the procedure with the rest of the mixture. These patties look like flapjacks and can be stacked for hungry eaters. Sometimes my wife and I cook this recipe for a light meal, folding the patties over and serving them with stir-fried vegetables and bread sticks.

Variations: Variations are endless. If you like Mexican or southwestern foods, add a minced jalapeño pepper or two. (Be sure to remove the seeds and inner pith unless you want the recipe very hot.) Fold these patties over, and top with freshly made salsa.

Bass Roll with Yellow Sauce

Here's a Colombian recipe that I have adapted, with some success, from *The South American Cook Book*. The white, flaky meat of the black bass is ideal for this dish. A 4-pounder is just right, but smaller fish will also work.

The Fish
4 pounds black bass (undressed weight)
water
milk
onion slice
sage
bay leaf
2 chicken eggs
1 tablespoon cornstarch
1 can kidney beans (16-ounce size)
parsley
2 carrots
bread crumbs
lemon or lime slices (for garnish)

Scale and gut the fish, leaving the head on. Cover the fish with water and a little milk in a suitable pot. (If you are using a single large fish, you may need to cut it in half to make it fit.) Remove the fish, and bring the liquid to a rolling boil. Add a bay leaf, a slice of onion, and a little sage. Put the fish back into the pot, and simmer until the fish flakes easily. While waiting, cut the carrots into strings. When the fish is done, remove it and flake the meat, discarding the bones. In a small bowl, beat the chicken eggs along with 1 tablespoon cornstarch, then mix into the flaked fish. Powder a large cloth napkin with bread crumbs. Spread the fish out on the bread crumbs. On top of the fish, spread out the kidney beans, sprigs of parsley, and carrot strings. Then shape everything into a roll, moving it to the edge of the napkin. Wrap the napkin around the roll, and secure it with cotton string.

Bring some salted water to a boil in a suitable container. (A large electric skillet will work.) Carefully put the fish roll into it. Reduce the heat, and simmer for 30 minutes. Meanwhile, prepare a yellow sauce.

The Sauce
1 cup chicken broth
1 tablespoon butter
1 teaspoon salt
1 teaspoon sugar
⅛ teaspoon white pepper
1 teaspoon minced fresh parsley
1 teaspoon cornstarch
2 beaten chicken egg yolks (large)
1 tablespoon vinegar

In a saucepan, heat the chicken broth, butter, salt, sugar, pepper, and minced parsley. Dissolve the cornstarch in a little water and stir it into the boiling broth. Reduce heat. Simmer and stir for 3 minutes. Add the beaten egg yolks, and stir until smooth. Remove from the heat, and stir in the vinegar. Unwrap the fish roll, pour the sauce over it, and serve, garnished with lemon or lime slices.

Note: Sticklers for South American chow might hold out for tapioca (made from cassava root, if it's *real* tapioca) instead of cornstarch.

Easy Bass au Gratin

Here's a recipe that works with a thick cream sauce (see chapter 11) or with a condensed cream soup, such as cream of celery. Be sure to try it.

2 cups cooked bass flakes
1 cup cream sauce or canned condensed cream soup
½ cup grated cheddar cheese
salt and pepper

Preheat the oven to 375 degrees. Grease a suitable baking dish. Mix the bass flakes, sauce or soup, salt, and pepper. Spread the mixture in the dish, sprinkle on the cheese, and bake for 20 to 25 minutes, or until the cheese is beginning to brown.

Bass Dressing

I like this dish by itself, but it can also be used as a dressing for roast turkey or pheasant. It's a good recipe for leftover bass, partly because it has a nice color in addition to flavor.

> 2 cups cooked bass flakes
> 2 cups corn bread and soft bread crumbs, mixed
> 2 tablespoons minced green bell peppers
> 2 tablespoons minced red bell peppers
> 2 tablespoons minced onions
> 2 tablespoons minced celery with leaves
> 1 tablespoon Worcestershire sauce
> 1 chicken egg, lightly beaten
> salt and pepper to taste
> milk

Preheat the oven to 350 degrees. Crumble the corn bread and shred the soft bread, mixing until you have 2 cups. Mix all the ingredients except the milk. Stir in enough milk to moisten the mixture nicely. Turn the mixture into a well-greased baking dish. Bake for 15 to 20 minutes, or until the top is slightly browned. Serve hot.

Black Bass Cheeseburgers

Here's a recipe to cook for folks who think they don't like bass. Kids are especially fond of these burgers.

> 2 cups cooked bass flakes
> 1 cup shredded cheddar cheese
> ¼ cup finely chopped green bell pepper
> ¼ cup finely chopped red bell pepper
> ½ cup finely chopped onion
> 2 tablespoons mayonnaise
> salt and black pepper
> 8 hamburger buns
> sauce of your choice (optional)

Preheat the oven to 375 degrees. Mix the bass flakes, cheese, bell peppers, onion, mayonnaise, salt, and black pepper. Divide the mixture into 8 equal parts, make patties, and sandwich them between the buns. Wrap each burger in aluminum foil, put them in the center of the oven, and bake for 15 minutes. Serve hot with potato chips or potato salad. I like to open my burger and spread on a little catsup or mayonnaise.

Bass à la Ghana

The peoples of Africa are fond of flaked fish, and their dishes are often served with a stiff porridge or rice. Although the conventional African recipes don't call for black bass, this fish is ideal for most of the dishes. Also, the largemouth has been stocked in many African impoundments and lakes in recent years, and smallmouth have been stocked in some of the streams. For this recipe I am indebted to *The Africa News Cookbook*. This book says that the fish can be baked or cooked by any method, but I like it sautéed in a little butter.

> 2 pounds black bass (undressed weight)
> 4 medium tomatoes, quartered
> 2 medium onions, quartered
> 1 to 2 tablespoons chopped chili peppers (deseeded)
> 1 teaspoon salt
> butter
> rice (cooked separately)

Using a blender or food processor, blend the tomatoes, onions, peppers, and salt until the mixture is smooth. (You can also use a mortar and pestle and lots of elbow grease.) Cut the bass into convenient-size pieces, and sauté in a skillet with a little butter until done. Flake off the meat in chunks (boneless) and mix gently with the tomato sauce in the skillet. Bring the mixture slowly to heat, but do not boil. Serve over rice.

Note: Be warned that the seeds and inner pith should be removed from the peppers unless you want the dish to be very hot. Also note that you can increase the amount of fish if you have plenty on hand. Most African folk recipes are designed to stretch out the meat or fish so that a little goes a long way.

Bass Scrapple

If you have a little bass left over from an evening meal, don't throw it out. Flake it off and make scrapple for breakfast.

> 1 cup cooked bass flakes
> 1½ cups fine-ground white cornmeal
> 1 teaspoon grated onion
> salt and black pepper
> ¼ teaspoon sage
> butter, cooking oil, or bacon drippings
> 4 cups water or mild fish stock

Mix the cornmeal, onion, and 4 cups of water or fish stock in a heavy boiler. Bring to a boil, then stir in the fish, salt, pepper, and sage. Cook and stir constantly until the mixture is thick. (The old rule is that it must hold the shape of a cross made on the surface with a spoon.) Pour and pack the mixture into a greased loaf pan or mold, then put it into the refrigerator to cool.

When you are ready to eat, slice the scrapple into ½-inch strips and fry it in butter or oil until it is browned on both sides. I like to cook a strip or two of bacon on a griddle, then use bacon grease for cooking the scrapple.

Note: If you boil fish heads and backbones in order to get a little meat for this recipe, be sure to save the liquid. Strain it and use it as part of the 4 cups of water.

EIGHT

Soups, Chowders, and Stews

Jackleg critics of the American culinary arts sometimes argue rather hotly over the merits of Manhattan versus New England fish chowders. Although not all of us have a ready supply of fresh Atlantic codfish, there is no need for the rest of the country to stay out of the fight. The plain truth is that the widely available black bass tops any fish that is normally used in either type of chowder. That's right. The ordinary black basses—both largemouth and smallmouth, as well as smaller cousins—have a mild, white flesh that flakes up just right, ideal for use in most fish chowders, stews, and soups.

Bass Head and Oyster Soup

I found this recipe in J. George Frederick's *Long Island Seafood Cookbook,* and I've used it to great advantage, in modified form. Of course, I cook it with heads of good black bass and prime Apalachicola oysters instead of with codfish heads and the fat mollusks of Long Island Sound. Since the Apalachicola oyster tends to be small, I have doubled the measure. In Frederick's text, it isn't clear to me what he finally does with the fish heads or the meat, although he definitely strains the broth and uses it in the soup. Well, I say, don't throw out the heads. If you don't want 'em in your soup, at least flake the meat off the throats and cheeks and add it to the soup.

98

3 or 4 bass heads (from 2- or 3-pound fish)
water
1 cup milk
2 dozen oysters (and liquid from shells)
1 medium onion, sliced
1 carrot, sliced
1 tablespoon minced fresh parsley
1 tablespoon butter
1 tablespoon flour
6 peppercorns, ground
salt and pepper to taste
mace

Wash the fish heads and shuck the oysters, saving all the liquid from the shells. Put ½ cup of oyster liquid aside and mix the rest (if any) with enough water to make 1½ quarts. Pour the liquid into a large pan, and add the fish heads, carrots, onion, peppercorns, and a pinch of mace. Bring to a boil, reduce heat, cover, and simmer for 2 hours. Remove the fish heads and drain. Strain the broth into another saucepan. Flake the meat off the fish heads, and add it to the new broth. Add the butter and the milk. In a small saucepan or bowl, dissolve the flour into the reserved ½ cup of oyster liquor, then stir the resulting paste into the soup. Increase the heat and stir until the mixture boils. Add the parsley. Season to taste with salt and pepper. Add the oysters, and simmer for 5 or 6 minutes. Serve with plenty of saltine crackers.

Variations: This recipe makes a rather thin soup. If you want it thicker, add more flour paste. You can also add diced potatoes and call the dish a chowder.

A. D.'s All-American Bass Chowder

Although this chowder recipe doesn't yet have a proper name, it does have flavor, aroma, good texture, and color. In short, it's a pretty dish as well as a tasty one. The recipe can be made with any good fish of mild flavor, but the black bass is perfect in both flavor and texture, provided that it isn't cooked too long or stirred too diligently.

> 4 or 5 pounds of bass (undressed weight)
> 3 strips smoke-cured bacon
> 1 large onion, chopped
> 3 cloves garlic, minced
> 1 tablespoon chopped parsley
> 1 can tomatoes (16-ounce size)
> 2 bay leaves
> salt and pepper

Instead of filleting the bass, scale and dress them whole. You can leave the skin on the fish, but if you want to remove it, it's best to skin the fish at the outset instead of scaling it. Remove the top and bottom fins by making a shallow incision down each side of the fins with a small, sharp knife blade and lifting out the fins and their bones. Be sure that *all* the bones come out with the fins. The chowder can also be made with fish fillets, but this process wastes some meat and robs the stock of some flavor.

After the fish has been dressed, fry the bacon in a skillet until it is crisp. Remove the bacon and drain. In the drippings, sauté the chopped onion for 3 or 4 minutes, then add the minced garlic and chopped parsley. Simmer on low heat for a few minutes. Meanwhile, put the dressed fish into a Dutch oven or similar pot, cover with water, and add the bay leaves. Bring to a light boil, reduce the heat, and simmer for about 10 minutes, or until the fish flakes easily when tested with a fork. Large whole fish will take longer than small ones or fillets. Remove the fish and drain.

While the fish are cooling down, pour all the liquid out of the pot, straining out and measuring 2 cups. (If you don't have 2 cups of stock, add a little water.) Discard the bay leaves. Put the 2 cups of liquid back into the pot, and add the contents of the skillet and crumble in the bacon. Chop up the tomatoes, and add them and the juice in the can to the pot. Put the pot on low heat, and stir in a little salt and pepper. Flake the meat off the backbones, watching carefully for bones around the rib cage, and add it to the pot. Simmer for a few minutes, but do not bring to a hard boil. Add a little more salt and pepper to taste, if needed, and stir *lightly* with a large spoon.

Serve the chowder hot in bowls, along with French bread or saltine crackers. This recipe will serve four or five people of modest appetite. If you want a larger batch, catch more fish and double the measures.

Variation: This chowder can also be made with the backbones, fins, and heads of a larger batch of bass that have been filleted. In fact, this version may even be better because the bones add to the stock—and it's bonus eating from scraps that are normally thrown away.

Proceed by boiling all the fish pieces (along with the bay leaves) in a little water for a few minutes. When the meat can be flaked off the backbones easily, remove them and drain on a plate. When they have cooled a little, pull off the fins and start flaking off the meat with a fork while the heads cook a little longer. (The heads are thicker and require longer cooking.) After about 20 more minutes, take out one of the heads and start flaking off the meat. You'll find that the throat contains quite a bit of meat of excellent quality, and the cheeks also contain some choice meat. In short, get whatever meat you can find. The tongue and the eyeballs are also edible, but suit yourself and your guests. (I always eat the tongue while flaking the meat off the head, and I save the eyeballs for my guest of honor.) Flake the heads one by one, then strain off and retain the broth. For the recipe above, you'll need about 3 cups of flaked fish from the backbones, fins, and heads. A little more or less will be satisfactory, but don't skimp too much. Fish flakes can be frozen for future use, so you can save up a batch whenever you dress fish. Be sure to also save some of the broth to go in the recipe. I put the fish flakes into a plastic container and pour the broth in with them before freezing.

Other Variations: The above recipe can be modified considerably to suit the occasion or your taste. Diced potatoes (as used in both New England and Manhattan chowders) will add bulk to fill up more people if you don't have enough fish to feed everybody, or if you are feeding Yankees. Half a cup of diced okra will thicken the dish into a gumbo, which can be served in a bowl over pre-cooked rice. And a few mushrooms sautéed along with the chopped onions won't hurt a thing. If you've got green onions, be sure to add some of the tops; these can be chopped and used instead of parsley. A few wild onions (or ramps) with green tops work wonders in this recipe, provided that you like onions with a strong flavor.

So, vary the ingredients at your culinary whim, but before you start cutting stuff out, remember that bits of stewed red tomatoes go nicely with the white fish flakes and specs of green stuff. Just be careful about what you call the results in mixed company—and be warned that Maine's legislature once deemed it illegal to put tomatoes into anything called a chowder.

Black Bass Bisque

Bisque, a popular soup that calls for cream or milk, always works best with a mild, flaky fish. Black bass are ideal. Although fish flakes and leftovers can be used for this dish, it is really better to cook the fillets in the soup, then break them up before serving.

> 1 pound bass fillets (skinless)
> 3 cups milk
> ½ pint cream
> ¼ cup sherry
> 3 tablespoons butter
> 1 tablespoon flour
> 6 green onions with part of tops, chopped
> salt and white pepper to taste
> paprika

In a Dutch oven or soup pot, melt the butter and sauté the chopped onions for 5 minutes, then remove them with a slotted spoon. Stir in the flour and cook, stirring constantly, for 3 minutes. Add the milk and sherry, stirring as you go, and cook almost to the boiling point. Turn the heat down to very low. Add the fish and onions. Cook and stir until the fish breaks up into pieces, about

10 minutes. Remove the pot from the heat. Stir in salt, white pepper, and cream. Transfer to a tureen and sprinkle the top with paprika. Serve hot with crackers.

Sow Bass Soup

The next time you catch a 5- or 6-pound bass full of roe, consider using the head and tail for this Viennese soup. If you fillet the fish, also include the backbone in this recipe.

> bass head, tail, and roe
> 7 cups water
> 1 cup red wine
> 1 medium onion, quartered
> 4 ounces fresh mushrooms, sliced
> bacon fat
> 2 tablespoons flour
> 2 bay leaves
> 3 peppercorns
> ½ teaspoon chopped fresh thyme
> salt

Put the water, wine, fish parts, onion, salt, peppercorns, bay leaves, and thyme into a suitable pot; bring to a boil, reduce heat, and simmer (at a light boil) until the liquid is reduced by half. This will take about 1 hour. While the pot simmers, heat the bacon fat in a skillet and stir in the flour; stir constantly for 10 minutes, then remove from the heat. Poach the roe in a little water in a saucepan, simmering for 10 minutes, then drain. Sauté the mushrooms in bacon grease in a small skillet for 6 or 7 minutes.

After an hour, remove the fish from the stock pot and strain the liquid. Put the liquid back into the pot, turn the heat up, and add the flour mixture, stirring for 2 minutes or so. Using a fork, pull the meat from the fish pieces and flake it nicely. Remove the skin from the poached roe, and separate the eggs. Add the bass flakes, roe, and mushrooms to the soup pot. Stir and serve hot.

Big Bass Stew

If you've got a stove-top Dutch oven, a large bass, a sack of onions, a slab of salt pork, a box of crackers, and some black pepper, you're in business. In my opinion, this is one of the best ways to cook a black bass that tips the scales at 8 pounds or better. Of course, smaller bass can be used if necessary.

> 1 large bass (8-pound size or better)
> ½ pound salt pork
> water
> 2 large onions
> black pepper
> crackers

Fillet the bass, and cut it into boneless chunks of meat. Save the backbone, rib sections, and throat. Dice the salt pork, and fry it in the bottom of a stove-top Dutch oven until it is browned. Cut 2 onions into ¼- to ½-inch slices. Place a layer of sliced onions over the salt pork. Add a layer of bass pieces. Sprinkle with freshly ground black pepper. Repeat the layers of onions, bass, and pepper until you run out of fish or reach the top of the Dutch oven. If you've got space left, lay the backbone, rib sections, and throat on top. (Do not mix these in; you'll need to remove them first in order to get all the bones out of the stew.) Add enough water to *almost*—but not completely—cover the ingredients. Bring to a boil, cover tightly, reduce heat, and simmer for 30 minutes, or until the fish is done. Do not stir. Take out the bony pieces, and pull off the meat with a fork. Add the meat back to the pot. Add some crackers to take up some of the moisture.

The texture of the stew is important; each serving should more or less stand on a plate. If all goes according to plan, the stew should be served in more or less pie-wedged-shaped pieces with a narrow spatula, going down deep enough to get some of the salt pork, with each layer distinct. For this reason, the stew should not be stirred while it's cooking. If it's too soupy, leave it on the stove without the lid for a few minutes. If it's still too soupy, eat it anyway. It will be very good, if not perfect in texture. Try again the next time you get a big bass.

Russian Soup

The Russians are fond of fish soup, and this dish, called *ookha*, is one of the very best. It is usually made with white-fleshed fish, and American bass are ideal. There are several variations on the dish, some of which call for strained broth. But I like some chunks of fish in mine, as reflected in the recipe below. The soup can be made with a large bass or more than one smaller fish.

    4 pounds bass (undressed weight)
    2 quarts water
    1 carrot
    1 medium onion
    1 parsnip
    1 celery rib with leaves
    juice of 1 lemon
    2 tablespoons sherry
    2 bay leaves
    10 peppercorns
    salt

Skin and dress the bass so that you have boneless fillets, leaving the backbone, rib cage, and fins intact. Set the fillets aside and put the bony pieces, including the head, into a large pot. Add the water, bay leaves, peppercorns, and salt. Bring to a boil, cover, reduce heat, and cook for about 30 minutes. Strain off the liquid and reserve; remove and drain the bony pieces, and discard the bay leaves and peppercorns. Return the liquid to the pot, and bring to a boil. Cut up the celery, carrot, onion, and parsnip, and add them to the pot. Simmer, covered, for 30 minutes. Meanwhile, use your fingers and a fork to pull the meat off the bony pieces of fish. Add the flaked meat to the pot, along with half of the fillets.

Cook until both fish and vegetables are tender, then strain off the liquid and reserve once again. Put the vegetables and fish into a food processor or blender for a few seconds. Put the strained liquid back into the pot, and add the processed fish and vegetables. Bring to a boil. Cut the remaining fillets into bite-size chunks, and add them to the soup. Cook for about 15 minutes, or until the fish is done. Carefully stir in the lemon juice and sherry. Serve in bowls, being careful that each serving gets a chunk or two of bass.

NINE

Campfire and Shore Lunch Bass

It's true. The best fish in the world are cooked beside a lake or stream. I'm especially fond of a bass shore lunch during a float-fishing trip in October or November, when the weather is usually perfect for a wood fire. Unfortunately, wood fires are not allowed on the shores of some of our lakes and impoundments. This is sad news for camp cooks, but on the other hand, modern gas-powered stoves are easy to use and most of them do a super job. Some of the best bass I've ever eaten were cooked by a small stream in Florida, in a cast-iron skillet heated by a gas cylinder on the tailgate of a pickup truck. A friend in Virginia argues that the best bass are cooked in midlake on a pontoon boat.

In any case, the new portable silo cookers and gas cylinder units add versatility to camp cooking, and many of the recipes presented in other chapters of this book will work in camp. It's best, of course, to choose recipes that require a minimum of time and a short list of easily transported ingredients.

Pea River Bass

In my neck of the woods, the time to hunt grapes is in September, or possibly the last week in August or the first week in October, depending on the weather. We have several kinds of wild grapes in this area, but my favorite is the bullace (or bullage, a wild muscadine), which grows all the way to the top of trees. Sometimes these large grapes can be taken from low-hanging limbs, but my guess is that most of them taken for human consumption are picked up off the ground.

Of course, these large grapes attract wildlife as well as people, and they often grow along streams. Find a good vine over a deep eddy hole of water or along an outside bend of the river, and you probably have a good catfish hole. My brother also has a theory that big soft-shelled turtles run up the small feeder creeks in the fall in search of these grapes.

In any case, bass fishing on a small stream in the fall is lots of fun and can be quite productive for largemouth, smallmouth, redeyes, or spots. This recipe is good for streamside cooking because it requires very little stuff to tote along and very little cleanup.

    stream bass
    wild bullaces
    butter or margarine (optional)
    salt
    heavy-duty aluminum foil

After you catch a bass of about 1 pound, find some bullaces, build a good fire, and let it burn down to coals. Clean the bass, cutting off the head and tail. Remove the fins so that they won't puncture the aluminum foil. When the coals are ready, tear off a sheet of foil and grease the center of it with butter, if you have it. Sprinkle the fish inside and out with a little salt. Put it onto the aluminum foil. Hold a bullace near the cavity, and pop it between thumb and forefinger so that the pulp plops into the cavity. Then put the hull in with it. Do this with several more, until the cavity is full. Then pop some more bullaces and put hulls and pulp beside the fish and on either end. Each 1-pound fish should have about a dozen bullaces. And don't forget the hulls. That's where the flavor is, as lovers of scuppernong hull pie know.

If you've got butter or margarine, put a little on top of the fish. Seal the foil with double folds, then rake some red-hot coals away from the fire. Put the fish onto the coals, and leave it for 30 minutes. Larger fish will take longer and may require more coals raked from the main fire. I like to build a fire with oak or other good wood, but it's easier and quicker to use charcoal if you want to haul it along. You can also cook this recipe on the patio, and, I might add, both bullaces and scuppernongs (a cultivated muscadine) are available in some supermarkets these days, or from home orchards.

Corn Shuck Bass Hobo

I have used several recipes for cooking small trout in corn shucks, and I can't argue with the results. For bass, however, I usually prefer to use aluminum foil along with the corn shucks, hobo-style.

> 1-pound bass
> 1 large potato
> 1 medium to large onion
> 1 tablespoon butter
> 1 tablespoon white wine Worcestershire sauce
> salt and pepper
> mushrooms or other vegetables (optional)
> corn shucks

If you are using dried shucks, soak them in water for 1 hour or so. Build a good wood or charcoal fire, and let it burn down to coals or, if your fire is large enough, rake some coals aside for cooking.

Scale, behead, and dress the bass. Leave it whole, but carefully cut out the top and bottom fins (so that they won't punch into the aluminum foil) and the bones associated with the fins (so that they won't punch into your gullet). Tear off a suitable length of aluminum foil, and spread it out. Arrange 2 or 3 corn shucks in the center of the foil. Cut the potato into ¼-inch slices, and arrange these on the corn shucks. Sprinkle the fish inside and out with salt and pepper, then put the butter inside the body cavity. Place the fish atop the sliced potatoes. Quarter the onion, and put half on one end and half on the other. Arrange the mushrooms and other vegetables on the ends and sides. Pour the white wine Worcestershire sauce over the fish. Top with another sheet of aluminum foil, then carefully seal the edges, best accomplished by first making a 2-inch fold lengthwise along one edge, then making a fold in the fold. Make a similar fold on the other side and on the ends. The essential idea is to seal in the steam to help cook the fish.

Put the package on the coals, and leave it for 20 minutes. Then carefully remove it from the coals, and let it sit for a few minutes to finish steaming. Note that this cooking time is for a 1-pound fish. Smaller fish will require less time, and larger ones more. When you open the package for eating, do so carefully, bearing in mind that the fish may have to be resealed and cooked longer if it isn't done. I've never had this method fail me, but I always worry about it.

Variations: You can also try asparagus spears, long green beans, or even broccoli. I like mushrooms in a bass hobo. If you've got fresh corn, put a roasting ear in with the fish if you've got room.

This recipe can also be used on the patio or on a kitchen stove-top grill. Place the aluminum foil directly onto the hot grill.

Grilled Bass

Long-handled, hinged baskets come in handy in camp, although they are a little awkward to tote about. In addition to being used as a hinged grill, which makes it easy to turn the fish, the basket can be unhinged and used as a grid for holding a coffee pot or a skillet over the fire. It's possible to use another type of grill for holding bass over a fire, but I really don't recommend it. The hinged grill's long handle enables you to remove it—and the fish—from the fire very quickly.

Almost any grilling recipe can be used over a campfire. Boneless fillets are much easier to cook than whole fish and require only 2 or 3 minutes cooking on each side. I am fond of grilling 10-inch bass whole, however, as in the recipe below.

> 10-inch bass (1 or 2 per person)
> bacon drippings or butter
> lemon (optional)
> salt

When your campfire coals are ready for grilling, grease the bass and sprinkle it with salt inside and out. Place the whole fish inside a greased grilling basket, and lock it shut. Put the fish about 5 inches above the hot coals, and cook for about 5 minutes on each side, basting once or twice with bacon drippings or butter and with a little lemon juice, if you have it. The fish should be done inside at the same time that it is nicely browned on the outside. This is not difficult, but experience at the grill is the best guide. You can test the fish with a fork without having to unhinge the basket; the fish is done when it flakes easily. The skin will sometimes start to break away from the fins when the fish gets done, but the old fork test is the best indication. If the fish seems to be getting brown too quickly, raise it higher above the coals.

Skillet-Fried Camp Bass

My favorite recipe—bass, cornmeal, salt, and hot peanut oil—is hard to beat for camp cooking (see A. D.'s Quintessential Bass in chapter 1). The only problem in camp is heat control. Wood fires get very hot, and sometimes it's not easy to handle the skillet. Your best bet is to make a main fire, then rake out some coals for cooking. A keyhole fire works well, with the wood in the larger end and the hot coals raked into the smaller end. Before building the fire, make the set and be sure that your skillet will sit level on the rocks. If you don't have rocks, try two green logs butted together, forming a V shape. A pair of chef's gloves, lined with asbestos, are helpful for handling a hot skillet.

Camp Fish Stew

Any good recipe for fish stew or chowder can be cooked in camp, if you've got all the stuff and a large pot. (It's best, however, to stay away from recipes that call for milk or cream.) Stew is an efficient way to cook for 6 or 8 people, if you've got that many to feed. This recipe contains lots of vegetables and can be served with crackers. I cook it in a Dutch oven.

5 or 6 pounds of bass (undressed weight)
¼ pound salt pork
2 cans tomatoes (16-ounce size)
3 medium potatoes, diced
3 medium onions, diced
3 carrots, sliced
2 tablespoons chopped watercress (optional)
1 green bell pepper, diced
black pepper
2 cups water

Dress the fish, producing skinless fillets. Cut the fillets into 2-inch pieces. Tie the bony pieces, head, tail, and skin into a piece of cheesecloth. Brown the diced salt pork in the Dutch oven. Remove the diced pieces and drain. Sauté the onions for 5 minutes in the salt pork fat. Add the potatoes, carrots, bell pepper, and watercress, along with the black pepper and salt pork pieces. Add 2 cups of water and the bag of fish heads. Bring to a boil, reduce heat, cover tightly, and simmer for 20 minutes. (Reducing the heat isn't so easy in camp, unless you've got a gas stove. When cooking over a fire, this usually can be accomplished by pulling the Dutch oven to one side of the fire, then raking away some of the coals. Or you can rig a tripod and suspend the Dutch oven over the fire, then raise it with a chain when you want to reduce the heat. In any case, don't boil all the water away. Add more water if you need to. After 20 minutes, remove the bag of bass pieces and discard them, or save them for nibbling. Add the tomatoes and bass fillets, then simmer for 10 to 15 minutes, or until the fillets flake easily. Serve hot with crackers. If you're really into camp cooking, you'll want to cook some fresh sourdough bread for this feast.

TEN

Bass Roe and Culinary Surprises

I'm putting this chapter toward the end of the book for two reasons. First, there's sometimes an advantage in saving the best for the last. Second, there is a practical consideration in that some Americans are not yet ready to stomach the best parts of the black bass and other good fish. I learned this while working on the first edition of my *Complete Fish & Game Cookbook*, first published by Outdoor Life Book Club. My editor, based in New York City, almost got sick while reading the text about fish liver and some other parts and wanted to cut out what I considered the best parts of the book—and some of the best eating. I explained to him that the liver of certain fish is considered to be a delicacy in other parts of the world, with the eelpout (or burbot) liver being highly prized in Scandinavia. Further, I went on, the liver of a largemouth bass is as good as that from a soft-shelled turtle. But perhaps I'd better start this chapter off with some good white-fleshed parts.

THROATS

The best piece of fish is often thrown away. This is especially true of black bass, grouper, red snapper, and similar fish with large mouths. Basically, the throat is a triangular piece of meat defined by the pelvic fins, the pectoral fins, and the gill plate. This piece of meat is usually cut off with the head and left attached to it.

If you are cooking the bass heads, as I highly recommend, you may choose to leave the throat intact. If you are frying, grilling,

113

or broiling fish, however, consider cutting out the throat and cooking it as a separate piece. To cut out the throat, force a sharp, heavy knife along the gill plate after the head has been cut off. The maneuver is not difficult, but the blade must be applied with force, and most fillet knives are too flimsy for this purpose. After you remove the throat, the two pelvic fins will still be attached. Leave these on. Skin the throat, and butterfly it by cutting a slash lengthwise on the inside. Skinning isn't absolutely necessary, but the throat is covered with tiny scales that are difficult to remove.

Once removed and skinned, the throat can be grilled, fried, or broiled along with the other fish. If you are fortunate enough to have a large batch, consider grilling them. Note that you can save up a batch by freezing then as you go along in containers partly filled with water. The smaller cylindrical plastic freezer containers are ideal.

Be warned that the throat has an unusual bone structure. It is not difficult to eat, but proceed cautiously until you are familiar with the lay of the bones.

In case anyone is skeptical about bass throats, I might point out that throats from red snapper and grouper are often sold in restaurants at fancy prices. In some cases, however, the fish mongers keep these choice pieces for themselves.

BASS ROE

Be careful when you gut a big bass. The sows get fat with roe shortly before going on the bed, and often the time of bedding can be unpredictable. The most intense bedding takes place in spring (or sometimes in February in Florida), but I've found roe in bass during every month of the year. I think they'll bed more than once during the year if food is available to feed more fish, and sometimes they also bed after a summer flood.

Roe is very good when properly fried or poached. Sometimes I'll freeze roe in small containers, covering them with water, until I get enough to cook separately. The roe should not be cut with a knife, and it should be removed with the two sacs joined. Puncturing or separating the sacs will allow some of the eggs to get out and complicate cooking.

Lagniappe Fry

In Cajun cookery, *lagniappe* means an unexpected treat. Bass roe fits this description exactly, and more often than not it is fried along with the fillets. In this case, it's easier to use the same coating and the same oil. Simply salt the roe sacs, shake them in cornmeal, and fry them for 3 or 4 minutes. Cooking them too long makes them dry. If you have enough bass roe to fry independently of the fish, try flour instead of cornmeal. A thick batter is not recommended for roe, at least not by me. Be warned that roe tends to pop in hot grease. It's probably best to cook the fillets first, then turn down the heat to cook the roe, but I confess that I usually fit the roe in around the pieces of bass. In any case, I do not recommend that you cover fish or roe while frying. I've suffered mild grease burns on my hands when I reached in to turn the fish or roe with tongs, so be cautious.

Sautéed Bass Roe

Whenever you have enough bass roe to make a meal, consider sautéing them in a little salted butter on low heat. No flour, cornmeal, or batter is necessary. As a variation, add a little lemon juice to the butter.

In some areas where cod, shad, or mullet roe are available commercially, or in quantity to the sportsman, chefs are fond of cooking and serving roe with bacon. Often the roe is first poached in water (with a little lemon juice) for a few minutes. This process expands the roe. Then the bacon is fried and the roe is sautéed in the drippings. The same techniques can be used for bass roe, but I usually omit the poaching step.

Bass Roe and Chicken Eggs

Break the roe sac and squeeze out all the eggs. Sauté these for a minute in butter, then add lightly whisked chicken eggs. Scramble until the chicken eggs set. Salt and pepper to taste. If you've got green onions, chop up one or two, with part of the green tops, and mix them in with the roe eggs. I like this dish made with a few wild onions. Most wild onions and garlics are quite strong, however, so proceed cautiously until you gain a feeling for the strength of the ones in your area.

Salt-Dried Roe

Often when I catch a bass with a nice set of roe about 3½ inches long, I wash it carefully without separating the sacs. Then I salt it down and place it on a brown grocery bag. The salt starts drawing out the moisture immediately. Within 1 hour or 2 hours, I move the roe to another part of the bag and add more salt. This goes on for several cycles (turning the roe with each new salting), until the salt no longer draws enough moisture to wet the bag under the roe. Usually, I let it sit for 2 days. Then I slice it very, very thinly and eat the slices atop thin crackers. Some people like a drop of lemon juice. Other people won't touch this stuff, saying that it isn't cooked. Well, caviar isn't cooked either.

BASS LIVER

Bass liver is very good. If I am frying freshly caught bass, I usually cook the liver along with the rest. If I do fry the liver separately, I normally use flour instead of cornmeal for coating. Sprinkle the liver with a little salt before dusting it with flour or cornmeal, then cook it quickly. Do not overcook. If you do, it will be hard.

When you dress the bass, be careful that you don't cut the liver. It is up toward the head and is often cut in half when you behead the fish. It's best to get it out in one piece, and then carefully cut away a sac that is attached to it. I don't know exactly what's in the sac, and I don't really want to know, but I think it's gall of some sort.

If you catch lots of bass and love liver, perhaps you'll want to cook a batch. Recipes especially for fish livers are hard to come by in the United States, but I have seen a few. Chicken liver recipes can be adapted, but remember that the liver from a 4-pound bass is a little smaller than that from a chicken. You can mix bass and chicken livers if you don't have quite enough, or you can freeze the bass livers (if they are very fresh) and save up a mess.

Bass Rumaki

In the classic rumaki recipe, a small piece of liver and a slice of water chestnut is wrapped with half a strip of bacon. Livers from large bass work fine, and 2 livers from smaller bass can be wrapped together. The unit is held together by round toothpicks or a skewer, then broiled or grilled over charcoal until the bacon browns. When the bacon looks ready to eat, the liver will also be ready. I like to sprinkle on a little salt and Hungarian paprika during the last few minutes of cooking, but this isn't necessary. If you don't have water chestnuts on hand, try a slice of Jerusalem artichoke or jicama.

HEADS AND TAILS

Bass heads contain some very good pickings, and they can be poached and eaten as is. Even the eyeballs are edible, but most people will want to remove these. Chapter 8 contains some excellent soup and stew recipes that make use of bass heads and tails, as well as the backbone and fins from fish that have been filleted. The flaked bass recipes in chapter 7 can also be made from meat picked off poached heads. And the heads and tails can always be used to make fish stock and sauces, as discussed in chapter 11.

The head contains two wonderful pieces of meat on either side, known as the *cheeks*. On large sea bass and groupers, these can be removed and eaten separately, but with black bass these choice parts aren't really large enough to fool with by themselves. It's best to get them when you pick the meat from the rest of the head. You'll find good meat in all sorts of places, and you may even find yourself eating the heads for their own sake instead of using them for flakes, soups, and stock. They are very good when simply boiled in slightly salty water, with or without a bay leaf or two.

Many people include the throat of the bass with the head, and it is usually cut off with the head. As stated earlier, it can be removed and cooked as a separate piece. And a very good piece it is.

BACKBONES

What's left after filleting and beheading a bass contains a limited amount of very tasty fish. If I'm frying bass, I usually fillet the fish by cutting through the rib cage, leaving only the backbone, complete with fins and tail. This piece I cut in half and fry crisply with the other pieces. My wife always wants them, saying they are her favorite parts. They are mighty good, especially with the tail and fins cooked crisply. To eat this piece of fish, you first bite off the crisp end of the tail. Then you bite off the crispy part of the upper and lower fins. Next, you carefully pull out the fins and associated bones. Then you hold the backbone between both hands and eat it like corn on the cob, pulling off the meat between your teeth, leaving only a clean skeleton.

OTHER PARTS

Some fish have swim bladders that are very good when fried, but unfortunately the black bass has no such edible organ. The eyes of the bass can be eaten, but most Americans (this author included) will pass on these delicacies. Leave them in the head, however, if you want them or intend to use them for shock value at the table. The tongues of some fish are also very good, but bass tongues are not ideal, in my opinion.

Mullet have a large organ similar to a gizzard, and some people in Florida and Europe are fond of eating them. I know from personal experience that the "gizzard," or gullet, of a black bass can also be eaten without ill effects. If you want to try one, split it lengthwise, or turn it inside out, and wash it under running water. It's a beautiful piece of white meat muscle, but it is tough and almost tasteless.

118

ELEVEN

Sauces, Go-withs, and Special Ingredients

"Help! Help!" I once cried while trying to get out of an old edition of *The Escoffier Cook Book*. I had gone to these pages for instruction on the making of a sauce Normande, but I was referred back and forth to various recipes and instructions for fumet, sauce velouté, a pale roux, and so on, which in turn sent me off to other pages. When I finally got out of the quagmire, I decided that Escoffier was playing some sort of culinary game with the reader.

Yet the truth is that many sauces are made with other sauces as a base, making it convenient, for the writer at least, to make cross-references from time to time. I therefore make no further apology for the recipes and cross-references below, except to say that I have tried to keep the list short so that one has to flip through only a few pages in either direction.

Seriously, the French are sticklers for complicated sauces, and they often serve them with sole. Since the black bass has a white flesh like the sole, it occurs to me that some of my readers might want to pursue this matter further. With this thought in mind, I have proceeded cautiously in the first part of this chapter with a few somewhat simplified French sauces. (If you want to make a career out of French sauces, get *Escoffier* or *Larousse Gastronomique* and a few pads of stick-on notes in various colors. These come in handy for flagging the pages so that you can find your way back to where you started from.) Most of these sauces are served over poached fish, a basic technique covered in chapter 3.

Court Bouillon

This is a basic French recipe for making a liquid in which to poach fish, after which the liquid can be used as fish stock for making various sauces. Recipes are quite numerous, usually containing onions, carrots, and celery. The liquid is strained and used to poach the fish. Often it is stored in jars for future use. The idea is used in many parts of the world to add flavor to fish. The court bouillon below—as good as any, I say—is an old New England recipe. The first three ingredients are set forth in equal measures, but any mix of these yielding a full cup will be satisfactory.

⅓ cup chopped onion
⅓ cup chopped celery
⅓ cup chopped carrots
1 tablespoon chopped fresh parsley
2 bay leaves
6 cloves
6 peppercorns
3 tablespoons butter
½ cup red wine vinegar
2 quarts water

Put 2 quarts of water into a stock pot and bring to a boil. Meanwhile, in a skillet, heat the butter and sauté the carrots, celery, and onions. Add the skillet contents and the rest of the ingredients to the boiling water. Bring to a new boil, and simmer for 30 minutes. Strain the liquid and use it immediately or store in jars, refrigerated. If you freeze the court bouillon, use plastic containers instead.

Fish Stock and Fish Fumet

A few of the recipes in this book, and a number in other books, call for fish stock or fish fumet. I like to make fish stock whenever I'm left with heads, backbones, and fins from filleting. Then I freeze it in 1-cup plastic containers for future use. (You can also freeze the bony pieces themselves and boil them later for stock.) This frozen stock can be used in recipes that call for fish stock, or you can improvise with it. For example, a cup of stock, a cup of flaked leftover fried fish, a chopped onion sautéed in a little butter, some chopped parsley, and salt and pepper to taste makes a wonderful hot soup for a rainy day.

The recipe below is pretty basic. You can add other vegetables, such as carrots or mushrooms, in small amounts if you'd like. Increase the measures if you have lots of fish on hand.

> 2 pounds bass heads, backbones, and fins
> 2 cups water
> ½ cup dry white wine
> 1 medium onion, quartered
> 1 stalk celery, chopped along with green tops
> 1 tablespoon chopped fresh parsley
> 1 teaspoon salt
> 10 peppercorns
> 2 bay leaves

Rinse the fish parts. Put the vegetables into the bottom of a stock pot, and add the fish parts. Add the water and wine then bring to a boil. Add the other ingredients. Reduce the heat, and simmer uncovered for 30 minutes. Let the stock cool a little, then strain it through a sieve. Strain it again through two layers of cheesecloth. Use it as needed or freeze it for the future. I usually throw out what's left of the vegetables—but I like to gnaw on the bass heads.

If your recipe calls for fish stock, you've got it. If the recipe, French or otherwise, calls for fumet, simmer the stock until it is reduced by half. Then you've got fish fumet.

Note that some of the sauces below are made with the aid of fish stock.

Sauce Velouté (or White Sauce) for Fish

This is a rather basic white sauce, or sauce blanche, made with the aid of fish stock. Sauce Velouté is often an ingredient, or base, for other sauces.

2½ cups Fish Stock (above)
2 tablespoons butter
2 tablespoons all-purpose flour
salt and pepper to taste
¼ cup minced mushrooms (optional)

Heat the butter in the top part of a double boiler. Add the flour a little at a time, stirring as you go, until you have a smooth mix with a hint of brown. Add the stock, stirring constantly with a wooden spoon until the sauce is thickened; make sure that the bottom part gets mixed about to avoid scorching. Add the minced mushrooms if desired, and salt and pepper to taste. Bring some water to boil in the bottom part of the double boiler. Put the saucepan on top so that it will steam. Cook on very low heat for 1½ hours, stirring from time to time.

Anchovy Butter

Here's an excellent spread, or thick sauce, for use on poached or broiled fish. I use the anchovy paste because it is so convenient to squeeze out a small amount.

¼ cup butter, softened
1 teaspoon anchovy paste
juice of ½ lemon
½ teaspoon brandy
2 or 3 drops Tabasco sauce

Mash the softened butter in a small mixing bowl until it is creamy. Stir in the rest of the ingredients. Serve at room temperature.

Hungarian Sauce

I like this sauce over broiled fish partly because of its flavor and partly because of its color. Be sure to use the mild Hungarian paprika. Spanish paprika makes a hot sauce.

> 1 cup cream
> ½ cup Sauce Velouté (page 122)
> 2 tablespoons mild Hungarian paprika
> 1 medium onion, minced
> 1 tablespoon butter
> salt to taste

Heat the butter in a saucepan and sauté the onion until it turns golden brown. Stir in the paprika and cook for 1 minute. Then, stirring as you go with a wooden spoon, slowly add the cream and Sauce Velouté. Do not allow the sauce to boil. Add salt, if needed.

Bercy Sauce

Here's a good sauce that can be used over poached or broiled fish. I also like it on sautéed fish patties. It can be made with either white or red wine.

> 1 cup Sauce Velouté (page 122)
> ½ cup Fish Stock (page 120)
> ½ cup dry white or red wine
> 4 tablespoons butter (divided)
> 1 tablespoon minced shallots
> 1 tablespoon minced fresh parsley

Sauté the shallots in 1 tablespoon of butter until they are opaque and soft. Add the Fish Stock and wine. Bring to a light boil, and cook until the liquid is reduced by half. Using a wooden spoon, mix in the Sauce Velouté and stir for 3 minutes over medium high heat. Remove the saucepan from the heat, then swirl in 3 tablespoons of butter. Sprinkle with chopped parsley and serve hot.

Sauce Normande

Here's a good sauce to serve over broiled or poached bass fillets. It's easy—if you've got the Fish Fumet and Sauce Velouté on hand.

> 1 cup Sauce Velouté (page 122)
> 1 cup Fish Fumet (page 120)
> ½ cup plus 4 tablespoons cream (divided)
> 3 tablespoons butter
> 2 tablespoons minced mushrooms

Simmer the Fish Fumet and minced mushrooms in a saucepan until the volume is reduced by almost half. Take the pan off the heat. Stir in the Sauce Velouté and ½ cup of cream with a wooden spoon. Stirring constantly, simmer, but do not boil, the sauce until the volume is reduced by half. (Stirring with the wooden spoon keeps the sauce from scorching on bottom and also helps control the heat.) Remove the sauce from the heat, and stir in the butter and 4 tablespoons of cream. Strain through a sieve and serve hot.

Sauce Aurore

Here's a colorful tomato sauce that goes nicely over poached white fish fillets and looks good in a serving bowl.

> 1 cup Sauce Velouté (page 122)
> ¼ cup tomato puree (or to taste)
> 1 tablespoon butter, cut into small pieces

In a small saucepan with a handle, slowly mix the tomato puree into the Sauce Velouté, tasting as you go, until you have it the way you want it. Bring to heat until it starts to bubble. Remove from heat and add butter, a small piece at a time, as you swirl the pan about. (Do not use a spoon to stir in the butter; you want the swirl.) Keep warm and serve warm. Reheating Sauce Aurore is a culinary sin.

Mustard Sauce

Here's a sauce that should be prepared shortly before serving and kept warm.

> 1 cup Sauce Velouté (page 122)
> ½ cup Fish Fumet (page 120)
> 1 chicken egg yolk
> 2 tablespoons butter
> 1 teaspoon prepared yellow mustard
> ½ teaspoon ground white pepper
> ½ teaspoon salt

Mix the egg yolk and Fish Fumet in the cold top pan of a double boiler. Add the Sauce Velouté and stir well. Cook directly over medium heat without boiling, stirring constantly until the sauce is thick enough to coat the spoon. Take the pan off the heat from time to time to prevent boiling. Stir in the butter. Add the mustard, salt, and pepper. Remove the pan from the heat. To keep the sauce warm until time to eat, bring a little water to boil in the bottom half of the double boiler. Put the sauce over the hot water and stir from time to time.

Maître D'Hôtel Sauce

Here's a popular recipe for saucing fried fish. It can also be used as a baste during the last minute of broiling or grilling fish. Note that the sauce requires no cooking.

> ¼ cup butter, softened
> juice of 1 lemon
> 1 tablespoon minced fresh parsley
> ½ teaspoon salt
> ⅛ teaspoon white pepper

Whip the softened butter in a small bowl. Stir in the salt, pepper, and parsley. Slowly stir in the lemon juice. Put the sauce into a gravy boat, and serve at room temperature over fried fish.

Sauce Meunière

This is a brownish sauce that goes nicely over fillets sautéed in butter. Sauté (or pan-fry) the fish as usual, then remove the fillets and add the other ingredients to the skillet. Or you may prefer to prepare the sauce separately. In either case, the butter should be browned slightly over the heat.

> 1 cup butter
> juice of 2 lemons
> 2 tablespoons minced fresh parsley
> salt and pepper to taste

Heat the butter over low heat in a small skillet until it begins to turn brown. Quickly remove the skillet from the heat and stir in the parsley, lemon juice, salt, and pepper. Stir for a minute, then return the skillet to the heat for a minute. Remove the skillet from the heat, but keep warm until you are ready to serve the fish.

Note: It's best to use salted butter for this sauce.

Caviar Butter

Here's an interesting garnish to serve with fish dishes. It's served cold in a mold or cut into various shapes.

> ¼ cup black caviar
> ½ cup softened butter
> juice of 1 lemon

Stir and whip the butter until it creams. Mix in the caviar and lemon juice. Turn out into a butter mold and chill until you are ready to serve.

Variation: Culinary sportsmen may want to use the roe of black bass instead of commercial caviar. It's certainly cheaper and more interesting—and may even be better. Take enough bass roe to yield ¼ cup. Break the roe into a bowl, and remove the skin and veins. Add some cold water and wash gently. Drain and wash gently again. Drain the roe and add 2 tablespoons of salt. Refrigerate overnight. Rinse and drain. Use the roe instead of the black caviar in the recipe.

Easy Butter Sauce or Spread

Here's an easy spread to use on broiled, baked, fried, or poached fillets. A little goes a long way, in my opinion. Fresh dill is better, but dried can be used if you reduce the measure by half.

> ¼ cup softened butter
> 2 teaspoons minced fresh dill

Stir the dill into the butter and let it sit for a while before using. This sauce or spread can also be refrigerated.

Variations: Use 1 or 2 cloves of crushed garlic instead of the dill in the recipe above; add more garlic to taste if you like. Also try 1 teaspoon of dry mustard instead of dill. Or 1 teaspoon of dried tarragon. You can also use margarine instead of butter.

Yogurt Sauce

Here's a recipe I enjoy when my wife goes on a diet. It can be used to advantage over poached or broiled bass, spread on after the fished is cooked.

> 1 cup plain low-fat yogurt
> 1 tablespoon honey
> 8 drops or more Tabasco sauce

Mix the yogurt and honey, then stir in the Tabasco sauce one drop at a time, to taste.

Variations: Try a combination of dry mustard and honey, adding mustard to taste; you can increase the honey to 2 tablespoons if you like. If you want a sauce that's pretty as well as tasty, mix some pomegranate syrup into the yogurt. Then spread the sauce on cooked fillets, and garnish with pomegranate seeds on the side. As you can see, the combinations are endless.

Hot Pepper Sauce

If you like hot stuff and have some peppers on hand, be sure to try this recipe. It can be cooled and served with steamed, poached, fried, or grilled bass. I like it with small grilled bass, used sparingly during the last moments of grilling.

> 1 cup minced hot peppers
> 1 cup finely diced onion
> 1 tablespoon olive oil
> sea salt

Seed the peppers and remove the hot inner pith. Heat the olive oil in a small skillet. Sauté the peppers and onion on very low heat until the mixture is mushy and thick. Stir in the salt, then cook for a few more minutes. Chill before serving with fish, or use warm as a last-minute basting sauce. This sauce is best if used right away, so mix a new batch every time you serve it. If you need only a small amount, cut the measures in half.

Low-Fat Tartar Sauce

There must be a thousand recipes for tartar sauce. Here's a good one without much fat. If you want some fat, use 1 full cup of home-made regular mayonnaise and omit the low-fat mayonnaise and the yogurt.

> ½ cup low-fat mayonnaise
> ½ cup low-fat yogurt
> 2 tablespoons finely chopped salad pickles
> 2 tablespoons minced green onions
> 1 clove garlic, mashed and minced
> 1 tablespoon finely chopped fresh parsley
> 1 teaspoon prepared yellow mustard

When you mince the onions, be sure to include about half the green tops. Mix all ingredients in a bowl, transfer the sauce to a serving container, and refrigerate for 1 hour or so before eating.

Salsa

Any good salsa can be used with fish. I often buy it in jars from the Mexican section of my supermarket, and sometimes I can find freshly made salsa in one of the refrigerated sections. The best, however, is made at home from garden-fresh vegetables. You really do need home-grown tomatoes, meaning those that have ripened in your area instead of being picked green and shipped in. If you can't find these, substitute canned tomatoes.

> 4 medium tomatoes, chopped
> 1 medium onion, chopped
> 1 small stalk celery with part of tops, chopped
> ½ green bell pepper, chopped
> 2 or more canned green chili peppers, minced
> ¼ cup olive oil
> ¼ cup red wine vinegar
> 1 teaspoon mustard seed
> 1 teaspoon powdered coriander
> salt and pepper to taste

Carefully remove the seeds and inner pith from the chili peppers. Mix everything in a nonmetallic bowl. Cover and refrigerate for at least 3 hours, stirring from time to time. This chunky salsa can be served as a relish to be eaten with the fish, or you can reduce it to a sauce. If you want sauce, zap the chunky salsa in a food processor. Put it into a saucepan, bring it to a boil, reduce heat to very low, and simmer for 5 to 10 minutes until it is slightly thickened.

Red Horseradish Sauce

Bottled horseradish sauces are readily available, but I think freshly grated horseradish is better. Horseradish root is now available in most large supermarkets, and many gardeners grow their own.

1 cup catsup
about 1 tablespoon grated horseradish root

Grate the horseradish on a fine mesh, or zap it in your food processor. Slowly mix the horseradish into the catsup, tasting as you go. Set the mixture aside for about 30 minutes before serving. This mix makes a very good dip for deep-fried fish.

Variations: If you want a white horseradish sauce, substitute mayonnaise for the catsup. If you want a pink sauce, use half mayonnaise and half catsup.

Hot Creole Sauce

Here's a sauce that makes a nice dip for fried fish fingers or a topping for poached or otherwise bland fish.

1 large tomato, peeled and chopped
1 large onion, peeled and minced
1 fresh chili pepper, seeded and minced
3 tablespoons olive oil
1 tablespoon vinegar
salt and freshly ground black pepper

Heat the olive oil in a small skillet and sauté the onion for 5 minutes. Add the tomato, chili pepper, salt, and black pepper. Cook and stir for 5 minutes. Stir in the vinegar, and serve.

Note: Be sure to wash your hands after seeding and mincing the hot pepper. Add more than 1 chili pepper if you want a very hot sauce, or reduce the measure to ½ pepper if you want a milder one. A good deal depends on the size and kind of pepper. My last batch of this recipe was made with a little round pepper grown from dried pepper that I found in a bag of mixed seeds packaged and sold as parrot feed; a Korean lady at the store where I bought the package said that the pepper was Korean. I don't know. The parrot wouldn't eat it, and my wife planted some of the seeds. The peppers are the size of a marble, tasty, and hot as hell.

Paprika Sauce

Hungarian paprika is not a hot pepper, but it does add a unique flavor to foods as well as adding a nice color. Spanish and Portuguese paprika are much hotter and must be used in small amounts, so they are not as functional as a coloring agent. In any case, a paprika sauce goes nicely with poached, grilled, or broiled bass.

¼ pound butter
½ teaspoon Hungarian paprika
salt (if the butter is unsalted)

Melt the butter in a saucepan. Stir in the paprika, and the salt if needed. Serve warm over cooked fish, or use as a baste during the last couple of minutes of broiling or grilling.

Easy Tempura Dunking Sauce

The Japanese are fond of frying shrimp and other seafood in a light, fluffy batter. This seafood is usually served with a warm tempura sauce. The dunking sauce also can be used with bass fried with any sort of batter or coating. Try it with fried bass nuggets or shrimp-size fingers cut crosswise from a fillet.

½ cup chicken broth
½ cup soy sauce
juice of 1 lemon

Mix the ingredients in a small saucepan. Heat almost to boiling, then remove from heat and steep for a few minutes. Serve hot or warm.

Catsup and Other Bottled Sauces

In all probability, more ordinary catsup is used with fish than any other sauce. At a fish fry, heavy eaters typically load up their plates with fried fish, french fries, and fried hush puppies. Then they squirt a blob of catsup onto the plate and dunk each bite of fish, potato, and bread into it. I object to this practice, because I like the taste of my hush puppies and fried fish, and I wish that people would at least taste these before dunking them into catsup. It's true that I sometimes dunk french fries into catsup, but never fish or bread, if it's cooked to my satisfaction. I do keep a bottle of catsup in the refrigerator—but I don't put it on the table unless somebody asks for it.

If you are a catsup eater, you'll have your favorite brand, or perhaps your favorite recipe if you make your own. (Anyone who grows lots of tomatoes during the summer will probably have a surplus and ought to look into homemade catsup.) In addition to the ordinary catsup, there are some interesting variations on the market, such as jalapeño catsup.

There are also many other prepared sauces—and we see more and more every year. Often these are on the hot side. Some of the hot ones are thin, such as Tabasco sauce. Others are thicker, with a catsuplike consistency, such as Pickapepper from Jamaica and Dat'l-Do-It from Florida. Most of these are packaged in small bottles and are rather expensive. On the other hand, a little goes a long way for most folks.

You can also buy bottled tartar sauce and various other mixes if you don't want to make your own. I've bought béarnaise sauce that was especially good with fish. Caper sauce and hollandaise sauce are also available. I suggest that you go to the biggest supermarket in your area and take a look at all the sauces on the shelves. Look also in the Mexican and Chinese food sections, as well as with the vinegars and in any sort of gourmet section. Some stores don't seem to know where to put all this stuff.

The epicures of imperial Rome were fond of eating a sauce called *garnum*, made from a small fish by that name. A culinary sport by the name of Apicius wrote a recipe for the stuff, but the directions are rather cryptic by modern cookbook standards. Back then, garnum was produced commercially, and the best reportedly came from Pompeii. It was actually made with other fish, such as sardines, just as most of the "sardines" sold in tins in America these days are really herrings. Essentially, garnum is made by salting small fish (maybe guts and all) and stacking them in a wooden barrel. What drips out is garnum, more or less. Some recipes say to use 2 pints of salt per peck of fish. Others say to leave the mixture in the sun for 2 or 3 months. Still others call for oregano and old wine. Suit yourself.

A similar sauce is used today as an ingredient in Worcestershire and perhaps other sauces, usually made from anchovies, and in a fish sauce that is very popular in Southeast Asia. It is called *nuoc mam* in Vietnam, *nam pla* in Thailand, *tuk trey* in Cambodia, and *patis* in the Philippines. The people in these countries use it in recipes and as a table sauce. Consequently, lots of the stuff is consumed. How much? I don't have recent figures, but according to *Food in History*, the countries known as French Indochina back in the fifties used 10 million gallons a year. That's a lot of fish sauce. Imported fish sauce can now be purchased in some of the larger American supermarkets and specialty shops, and sometimes by mail order.

Coconut Milk

The coconut is now used in one way or another in the cuisine of most parts of the world, and coconut milk is a very important ingredient in many recipes of Africa and Indonesia. Many people who purchase coconuts at the supermarket think that the liquid inside, drained out by punching through one of the eyes with an ice pick, is coconut milk. It isn't. I've even seen articles that said this liquid is coconut milk. It isn't.

To obtain milk, you must first crack the coconut, remove the meat in chunks, and grate it. Measure the grated meat, and put it into a suitable container. Then pour over it an equal volume of steaming hot water. Let this steep until it is cool enough to squeeze the coconut meat in your hand. Then squeeze out the liquid and strain it. This is coconut milk. You can repeat the process several times, but note that the liquid will become weaker as you go. This weaker milk can be used to advantage when cooking rice, which usually goes with every Indonesian meal and with many African dishes. You can even obtain "cream" by letting the strong milk stand for several hours and then skimming off the rich top layer. You can also obtain a richer coconut milk by using hot milk (from a cow, yak, goat, camel, or water buffalo) instead of water.

For 1 cup of coconut milk, start with 1½ cups each of grated coconut meat and hot water.

If you don't want to bother with fresh grated coconut milk, you can substitute unsweetened desiccated grated coconut, available in packages at most supermarkets, or you may find canned or frozen coconut milk in supermarkets and specialty food stores. I have bought it by mail.

Marinated Jicama Chips

These crunchy chips are very easy to prepare and can replace the salad in a fried-fish meal. The jicama is a turniplike tuber from Mexico, and it is finding its way into American supermarkets, specialty markets, and even home gardens. It can be eaten raw or cooked. I like the following raw marinated version with fried bass. It has a light, refreshing taste that goes nicely with heavy fried fish.

> 1 jicama
> ¼ cup olive oil
> 2 cloves garlic, pressed
> 1 tablespoon chopped fresh cilantro

Peel the jicama and slice it thinly. Mix the olive oil, garlic, and cilantro, then marinate the jicama slices for about 2 hours. Serve cold with hot fried fish and corn bread.

Note: Also try some other good Latin American dishes with fried fish, such as sautéed cassava or plantain chips.

APPENDIX A

Ten Steps to Better Bass

We often hear from health-food experts that we should eat more fish—but we also hear, sometimes from the same experts, that we should not buy fish that smell fishy, have eyes that aren't bright, and so on. Clearly, the person who shops in a fish market has some sniffing around to do. I might add, however, that most people in this country never see the eyes of the fish they eat. Many supermarket fish these days are dressed before they are packaged for sale or put on display.

The person who catches his own fish has (or can have) the best of it from a culinary standpoint. Although black bass keep very well, compared with some soft-fleshed fish, the cook can do a better job if the following rules are followed.

1. Start with fresh fish. If you catch your own fish, you'll generally have full control of the important preliminary steps to culinary excellence. It's usually best to cook a bass shortly after it is caught. Out of the water and into the frying pan isn't necessary, however, for bass keep a good deal better than some other fish. And it is possible to keep bass alive on a stringer or in a live well. The best kind of stringer is the snap type, in which a sharp prong is run through the soft area of both the upper and lower lips rather than a cord being run through the gills. The snap is especially good when you have several bass on one stringer. If you use a live well, make sure the fish has plenty of oxygen or a steady supply of fresh water. I like an aerated system, but other rigs will also work if they are properly used. When running your boat at high speed, be sure that the live-well plug is in place so that the fish will have water.

In general, I prefer an ice chest to either a live well or a stringer. It's best to keep the fish on top of the ice, if possible, or to keep the water drained from the bottom of the ice chest. But I'm not a stickler on this point, and I have no real objection to keeping bass in ice slush. I've kept undressed bass on ice for 2 days without a problem.

If you start off with very fresh bass, you can keep them in the refrigerator for 1 or 2 days. But I prefer to freeze mine if I don't intend to eat them within 24 hours.

2. Field-dress the fish if necessary. If you can't keep the bass alive or on ice, it's best to stun them with a blow atop the head and draw them as soon as they are caught. Then keep them in a creel or arrange some means of cooling them by evaporation, if possible. Keeping them in damp moss in a breeze, thereby making use of evaporative heat loss, will lower the temperature quite a bit.

It might well be better to draw fish that are to be kept on ice, but I seldom go this far with black bass. In fact, if I have live or very fresh fish to work with, I often freeze them whole without even gutting them. Leaving the scales and skin on the fish helps prevent freezer burn. There are other advantages to this method that I'll discuss later.

In short, bass that are taken out of the water, stunned, and put immediately on ice do not have to be field-dressed. The key here is putting the fish on ice immediately, without allowing it to warm up.

3. Freeze quickly, thaw slowly. If you are going to freeze the fish, do so as soon as possible. It's best to freeze fish in a block of ice, usually by filleting or pan-dressing them and putting the pieces into suitable containers. (Half-gallon plastic milk cartons work nicely.) More and more, however, I lean toward freezing the whole fish—head, scales, and guts—in one piece. This method gives me several options when dressing the fish for cooking.

Some people recommend glazing a whole fish with a thin coat of water, but I seldom do this with bass. If you do glaze, it's best to get the fish ice cold and then coat it with ice water. Freeze it hard, then quickly glaze it again with ice water. After glazing, put the whole fish into the freezer for an hour or so to set the glaze. Then wrap the fish in plastic foil or freezer paper or both.

Despite expert advice to the contrary, I thaw out 95 percent of my fish in the kitchen sink instead of in the refrigerator. This is a practical matter, as it takes a whole fish—or a half-gallon jug of ice—a good long time to thaw out in the refrigerator. I have even had to use warm water in the sink more than once, and in a pinch I've used the microwave. But it really is best to thaw the fish slowly, if you have the time to wait for it to thaw.

4. Clean and dress the fish appropriately. Bass can be fried whole, with or without the head. These are much easier to eat if you remove the top and bottom fins and the associated bones. Cut around the fins on each side with a small, sharp knife, then lift them out. Each spiny ray that sticks up should have a corresponding bone that goes down into the fish. Removing these fins and bones makes the fish much easier to eat with a fork, by hand, or perhaps with chopsticks if you are cooking Chinese. (The Chinese are fond of cooking whole fish.) If properly prepared, small whole bass can be eaten quite easily by holding them like corn on the cob.

Bass for frying are usually filleted or pan-dressed. Fillets may or may not include the rib cage. I usually include the rib cage and cut the fillet in half or in three pieces. The bottom half is boneless, and a thick piece cut from the top of the rib cage is also boneless. The rib cage has plenty of bones, but I save these pieces for myself, as I know how to strip them in short order. By dividing the fillets into three parts, I have four pieces of boneless fish from each bass. I also cut the backbone in half, resulting in, along with the ribs, four pieces with bones, plus the throat, which I almost always use. These bony pieces fry up crisply, and my wife's favorite piece of fish is the backbone. These are, I might add, quite easy to eat once you have the hang of it, and the large bones are no problem for accomplished fish eaters.

I call this the Livingston method, designed to yield the maximum amount of boneless bass while wasting almost nothing. Most people who pan-dress a fish, however, will merely cut the fish in half lengthwise, then cut each piece in half. This will yield only one boneless piece. (I have also eaten fish that were cut crosswise, without *any* boneless parts.) This method is satisfactory for most people, and I sometimes use it with small bass. But if you have children or guests, go for four boneless pieces from each fish.

Steaks can be made from a large bass, but I seldom do it. I would recommend that the steaks be cut exactly 1 inch thick so that they can all be cooked the same length of time. Use an electric meat saw. The texture of bass steaks, I might add, is surprisingly different. Be sure to remove the fins and associated short bones before steaking the bass.

As a rule, pan-dressed fish are best for frying or grilling. Fish stews and casseroles are harder to eat if they contain bones.

I seldom skin a bass. The often repeated charge is that the skin of the bass imparts a muddy or bitter taste to the fish—but this I simply do not believe. In fact, the skin helps the flavor quite a bit by holding in the juices. If you are feeding New York outdoor writers or editors, or someone who objects to the skin for one reason or another, consider using a recipe that calls for skinned or flaked bass.

I like to freeze bass whole so that I can dress them according to the way they will be cooked when I'm ready to use them.

5. Choose a recipe appropriate to your guests. The worst thing you can do for a queasy eater is to serve up a 10-pound largemouth, baked whole, complete with head and tail and fins. Skinning the thing and removing the eyeballs won't help very much. Some people simply don't care for fish that look like fish. In this case, it's best to resort to the flaked bass recipes, which don't suggest fish at all. Try an au gratin dish, a casserole, or a bass-flake cheeseburger. And don't serve it up on a fish-shaped platter.

6. Do not overcook bass. If fried too long at a low temperature, bass becomes dry and chewy. Bass cooked under a broiler or over a grill also become less than succulent when cooked too long. (In this regard, some of the fatty fish are more forgiving.) Exact cooking is more art than science, but the ideal is to have a perfect combination of fish thickness and heat, allowing the outside to become nicely browned just as the inside is cooked through. There is some leeway—but not much with bass cooked by a dry heat method.

7. Do not serve greasy or smelly fish. An important part of frying is to drain the food properly. A brown bag works fine, if the fish or other fried foods are not overlapped. Never pile the fish onto a platter or plate to drain; the bottom will wind up too greasy. If you do have to pile or stack fish, drain them first on a brown bag.

Some people object to the smell of fish in the kitchen and house. I don't have this problem, but more than one of my guests has commented that the down-sucking vent system on my kitchen range is nice because it keeps the fish smell out of the house. Well, maybe this is a consideration, and I have known more than one man who had to cook the fish outside and bring them into the house in order to keep the peace.

8. Serve appropriately. At my house, fish, hush puppies, and fried potatoes are normally served atop a brown bag, or perhaps two or more brown bags, depending on how many people are being fed. Sometimes the brown bags are placed on large trays. Of course, this is finger food and the atmosphere is casual. Or should be.

If you want to dress for dinner and set a fancy table, don't cook fried bass. Go with poached fish, French sauces, and fancy trimmings. Don't serve on the patio. Break out the linen table-cloth and light the candles. Also, don't mix fish with other meats, unless you orchestrate separate courses. It's almost always a mistake to put fried bass on the same table with a roast turkey. Always try to have something unusual, such as sliced raw Jerusalem artichokes, that isn't really necessary for the meal. In season, we have hundreds of large pears on our trees. I peel and slice these to serve with fried fish, making a nice, light touch for an otherwise heavy meal.

9. Drinks and garnish. Garnish for flavor and color. Yellow lemon wedges go nicely with almost any fish dish, and mixing in some green lime wedges is a nice touch, even when you serve on a brown bag. If your setting is on the formal side, catsup and bottled sauces of various sorts look better when served in bowls.

The drink can be very important in a fish dinner. A white wine really helps poached fish but is too dainty for a fish fry. If you are serving piles of fried fish, it's hard to beat plain ice water or iced tea, the latter served in tall glasses with sprigs of fresh mint. I also like beer with fried fish, but, unlike beer connoisseurs, I want mine ice cold. A tall glass of cola or lemonade served on ice also hits the spot, especially with the kids.

Many people believe that drinking milk with fish can be dangerous to your health. I was brought up with this belief, and even today I simply don't want milk with fish of any sort, even though I have no objection to a nice thick cream sauce served over poached fish.

10. End with a nice touch. One of the best fish fries I ever attended was at the home of friends, where they fed about 50 people with the usual fried catfish, hush puppies, potatoes, and coleslaw on tables in the backyard. The fish were good— small fork-tailed channel cats about 8 inches long—and I ate far too much. What I really remember, however, is that the lady of the house came around at the end of the meal with a large tray piled high with wet, steaming cloth napkins—just right to get the fish grease off your hands. It was a very nice touch.

APPENDIX B

The Kinds of Bass

Hundreds of different sorts of fish are called bass, and some true bass are called something else. I don't have much of a guilty conscience about using a title that will be somewhat misleading to some people, because most of these recipes can be made with just about any fish called a bass. I could have narrowed the field down in the title, calling the book *Black Bass Cookbook*. The trouble here is that most of the people who catch black bass don't call them that and might not even recognize their favorite fish in the title. Thanks in part to large professional bass tournaments and media coverage, almost everybody who fishes very much in fresh water these days refers to the black bass simply as bass.

Those people who confuse the bass of my book's title with the various sorts of bass and so-called bass available at fish markets and in cookbooks do have a legitimate gripe. They should know that the black bass is not normally sold at the market, although it may be legal in some states to sell black bass from farm ponds. But because the black bass is now available for the catching to people in all states except Alaska, as well as in Canada, Mexico, South Africa, and many other parts of the world, I'm not about to offer a refund. If this book will introduce just one reader to the culinary merits (and ultimately to the sporting qualities) of the largemouth or smallmouth bass, then I'll sleep soundly at night.

To list and sort out every fish that is called a bass would take a whole book, but here's a short breakdown that I hope will be useful.

Black Bass. These include the largemouth and smallmouth bass, as well as the spotted bass (or Kentucky bass), and the redeye. There are several other species, or subspecies. The Florida largemouth, which attains a weight of over 22 pounds, is native to central Florida, but it has now been successfully stocked in other areas. The Suwannee bass, another Florida native, is limited to the Suwannee River drainage across north-central Florida. The Neosho smallmouth lives in a few tributaries of the Arkansas river in Arkansas, Oklahoma, and Missouri.

Most of the various black basses have local names, with the redeye being called Flint River smallmouth (in parts of Georgia), Chipola bass (in northwest Florida), and so on. And of course, the largemouth and smallmouth are also called bucketmouth, linesides, trout, green trout, bronzebacks, and so on. To straighten all this out would require an act of Congress, and probably the U.S. Army would have to be called in to force the people of Kentucky to call the spotted bass a spotted bass instead of a Kentucky bass.

In any case, all black bass are excellent eating, and there is no appreciable difference among species. As a general rule, the smaller black bass make the better eating.

Sea Bass. Most of the sea basses, including some giants, have mild, white flesh, rather flaky and low in fat content, and thus most of the recipes in this book can be applied to them. The large family of sea basses includes the grouper, the jewfish, and other saltwater fish. It can be difficult to identify among the various species of sea bass. Some of them look quite like the black bass. It's been said that Junior Samples of Hee-Haw fame got his start in show business by duping some Atlanta sports writers into thinking that the head of a large grouper from the Gulf of Mexico was from a world's record largemouth that Junior had caught in a Georgia lake.

I looked in several books for a fish that I call kelp bass. *The New Fisherman's Encyclopedia* lists the fish as California kelp bass, also called rock bass and sand bass. *McClane's New Standard Fishing Encyclopedia* has no entry for kelp bass or California kelp bass, nor is this fish discussed under rock bass, which is devoted to the small freshwater sunfish. *McClane's* does discuss the fish under sand bass, however, saying that the sand bass is often lumped with a very similar species, the kelp bass. Most freshwater anglers, however, know the sand bass to be the small freshwater white bass.

Striped Bass and Freshwater Cousins. The *Morone* genus includes the famous saltwater striped bass, which has become landlocked in some areas, as well as the small freshwater white bass, white perch, and yellow bass. All of these also have other names. The large striper is often called rockfish, and the small white bass is often called sand bass. The yellow bass is called barfish, brassy bass, stripe, striped bass, and streaker. Modern fishery biologists have even come up with a hybrid between the large striped bass of salt water and the small white bass of fresh water. In Florida, the hybrid is called sunshine bass.

All of these fish are edible. The yellow bass and the white perch are especially good.

Rock Bass. The rock bass is a small sunfish, and not a black bass, although it is often caught in bass waters. The rock bass is fairly good eating, but in my opinion it's not as good as a black bass. Several similar species, such as the warmouth, live in various parts of the country.

Cookbook Bass. Unfortunately, the term *bass* as used in most cookbooks refers to something other than the freshwater black bass. Even the term *black bass* usually refers to a sea fish, or black sea bass, *Centropristis striata;* this bottom fish averages about 2 pounds and is very popular along the Atlantic seaboard from Massachusetts south. In New York, the Chinese love to steam this fish whole. (See the recipe on page 34.) Some of the other sea basses are very good when fresh. In Europe, the term *bass* usually refers to the *Morone labrax* species, which is highly prized.

A few cookbooks do refer to the freshwater black bass, but the coverage is usually quite limited and often lacking. One book, for example, allows that the black bass is fun to catch while ice fishing. Well, maybe. But the bass is a warmwater species and slows down in cold water, and catching one through the ice is about like pulling in a stick. For a real understanding of the black bass, forget about ice fishing; instead, cast a large rubber-legged deerhair bug into a pocket in the lily pads, let it sit perfectly still for a few moments, and then hold your breath as you twitch it gently. . . .

APPENDIX C

Metric Conversion Tables

U.S. Standard measurements for cooking use ounces, pounds, pints, quarts, gallons, teaspoons, tablespoons, cups, and fractions thereof. The following tables enable those who use the metric system to easily convert the U.S. Standard measurements to metric.

Weights

U.S. Standard	Metric	U.S. Standard		Metric	
.25 ounce	7.09 grams	11	ounces	312 grams	
.50	14.17	12		340	
.75	21.26	13		369	
1	28.35	14		397	
2	57	15		425	
3	85	1	pound	454	
4	113	2		907	
5	142	2.2			1 kilogram
6	170	4.4			2
7	198	6.6			3
8	227	8.8			4
9	255	11.0			5
10	283				

Liquids

U.S. Standard	Metric	U.S. Standard	Metric
$1/8$ teaspoon	.61 milliliter	$3/8$ cup	90 milliliters
$1/4$	1.23	$1/2$	120
$1/2$	2.50	$2/3$	160
$3/4$	3.68	$3/4$	180
1	4.90	$7/8$	210
2	10	1	240
1 tablespoon	15	2	480
2	30	3	720
$1/4$ cup	60	4	960
$1/3$	80	5	1200

To convert	multiply	by
Ounces to milliliters	the ounces	30
Teaspoons to milliliters	the teaspoons	5
Tablespoons to milliliters	the tablespoons	15
Cups to liters	the cups	.24
Pints to liters	the pints	.47
Quarts to liters	the quarts	.95
Gallons to liters	the gallons	3.8
Ounces to grams	the ounces	28.35
Pounds to kilograms	the pounds	.45
Inches to centimeters	the inches	2.54

To convert Fahrenheit to Celsius: Subtract 32, multiply by 5, divide by 9.

Index